Mothering and Mother(Work) in the Times of Black Lives Matter

Edited by Haile Eshe Cole, Shana Calixte Pitawanakwat, and Luciane Rocha

DEMETER

Mothering and Mother(Work) in the Times of Black Lives Matter
Edited by Haile Eshe Cole, Shana Calixte Pitawanakwat, and Luciane Rocha

Copyright © 2025 Demeter Press

Individual copyright to their work is retained by the authors. All rights reserved. No part of this book may be reproduced or transmitted in any form by any means without permission in writing from the publisher.

Demeter Press
PO Box 197
Coe Hill, Ontario
Canada
K0L 1P0
Tel: 289-383-0134
Email: info@demeterpress.org
Website: www.demeterpress.org

Demeter Press logo based on the sculpture "Demeter" by Maria-Luise Bodirsky www.keramik-atelier.bodirsky.de

Printed and Bound in Canada

Cover image: *Eternal Embrace* by Heather Lynch
Cover design: Michelle Pirovich
Typesetting: Michelle Pirovich
Proof reading: Jena Woodhouse

Library and Archives Canada Cataloguing in Publication
Title: Mothering and mother(work) in the times of Black Lives Matter / edited by Haile Eshe Cole, Shana Calixte Pitawanakwat, and Luciane O. Rocha.
Names: Cole, Haile Eshe, editor. | Calixte Pitawanakwat, Shana, editor. | Rocha, Luciane O., editor.
Description: Includes bibliographical references.
Identifiers: Canadiana 20250111721 | ISBN 9781772585322 (softcover)
Subjects: LCSH: Motherhood–Political aspects. | LCSH: Motherhood–Social aspects. | LCSH: Black lives matter movement. | LCSH: African American mothers. | LCSH: African American mothers–Political activity.
Classification: LCC HQ759.M68 2025 | DDC 306.874/308996073–dc23

The publisher gratefully acknowledges the support of the Government of Canada

To our mothers,
othermothers,
community mothers,
and caretakers
whose love has and continues to sustain us.

We are forever grateful.

May your spirits live on in us.

Contents

An Introduction
Haile Eshe Cole, Shana Calixte-Pitawanakwat, and Luciane Rocha
11

Section I
**Education: "Firm When It's Necessary,
Your Words Be Understood"**
27

1.
Mother and Child
Artwork by Devynity
28

2.
Freedom Choices: How Black Mothers Living in
the Jim Crow Era Protected Their Children From Anti-Black Racism
and Prepared Them for Success
*LaShawnDa Pittman, Alana Lim, Ayan Mohamed, Mia Schuman,
Rachel Vulk, and Rina Yan*
31

3.
A Lesson I Did Not Teach
A Poem by Jameka Hartley
65

4.
Known Black
A Poem by Jameka Hartley
67

5.
Nana Would Pull Magic from Out Her Pocketbook
A Poem by Devynity
69

6.
Mama Illusion
A Poem by Toya Leigh Groves
71

Section II
Motherwork: "You Will Protect Me with Love"
73

7.
Dear Mama
A Poem by Alexis Henderson
75

8.
Hard Questions
Traci-Ann Wint
77

9.
Ay-Yai! Black Mother Leadership and Storytelling Traditions
Stephanie Fearon
79

10.
Does Anyone Else Care? Black Mothering in the
Time of COVID-19 and Black Lives Matter
Chelsi West Ohueri
97

11.
Thank God for Aunties
A Poem by Devynity
103

12.
The Light We Carry: An Interview with Heather Lynch
Haile Eshe Cole
105

13.
For You, Infinitely
Adriel Michelle Barnett
119

Section III
Violence and Trauma: "Rinsing Pain and Casting Wishes"
127

14.
Almost Human
Photography by Haile Eshe Cole
129

15.
Conto De Cantos Chorados (A Tale of Crying Songs):
A Single Mother's Experience
Cynthia Rachel Esperança
131

16.
The Occlusive Carceral Tactics of White Womanhood
Erica Ewa-Elechi and Joshua Harris
137

17.
"I Beat Yo' Ass": Spanking in Multigenerational Immigrant Families
Christina Santi
159

18.
fire's rose
A Poem by Toya Leigh Groves
169

19.
One Day at a Time
Photography by Luciane Rocha
173

20.
Finding Joy in His Joy
Photography by Luciane Rocha
175

Part IV
Resistance: "I Know I'm Not the Only One"
177

21.
Protest! Mothering by Example
Photography by Luciane Rocha
179

22.
"I Am Parenting Black Children for the World": Black Mothers' Insights on State-Sanctioned Violence and the Fight for Black Lives
Seanna Leath, Dawn Demps, and Johari Harris
181

23.
The Judicialization of Black Suffering: Black Motherhood and the Criminal Justice System in Rio de Janeiro, Brazil
Luciane Rocha
199

24.
The Revolution Will Be Black, Queer, and Mother Led: Reflections on Seven Years of Mothering
Pascale Ife Williams and Johnaé Strong
219

25.
Motherhood in the Land of Hope
Jameka Hartley
231

26.
My Afro-Cultural Renaissance
A Poem by Azenia Whitaker
237

27.
Soiled Bandanas
A Poem by Toya Leigh Groves
241

28.
at the march for George Floyd
A Poem by Toya Leigh Groves
243

29.
The Dead Have a Voice
Photography by Luciane Rocha
245

30.
Investigate!
Photography by Luciane Rocha
247

Notes on the Contributors
249

An Introduction

Haile Eshe Cole, Shana Calixte-Pitawanakwat, and Luciane Rocha

"Mama!"

—George Floyd, 2020

The Black Lives Matter (BLM) movement began in 2013 as a response to the acquittal of George Zimmerman after he brutally murdered Trayvon Martin, a young, Black, and unarmed teenager. Founded by three Black organizers—Alicia Garza, Patrisse Cullors, and Opal Tometi—BLM grew into a global movement that both acknowledged Black humanity and called for an end to the unrelenting state sanctioned violence against Black bodies. Black Lives Matter protests erupted across the globe in response to the murder of yet another unarmed Black man, George Floyd, in Minneapolis—on the heels of the murders of Breonna Taylor and Ahmaud Arbery.

In parallel, anti-Black violence in Turtle Island has brought many to rage and resistance, including those of us in what we now call Canada. In that respect, a similar, albeit unique trajectory can be seen for developing the Black Lives Matter movement north of the United States (US) border. Moved to action by the murders of those in both the US and Canada, four activists in Tkaronto (Toronto)—Sandy Hudson, Yusra Khogali, Janaya Khan, and Pascale Diverlus—strategized to make the realities of anti-Black violence and racism seen and heard in the Canadian context. Their work builds on earlier actions against white supremacist police forces, such as the Black Action Defence Committee (BADC) work with activists Dudley Laws, Charles Roach and Sheorna Hall.[1] Focusing on education, the arts, decolonization and the fight for queer and trans rights, Black Lives Matter—Canada continues to spread across the country, with chapters in Vancouver, Montreal, Fredericton, London, and Sudbury.

In 2023, Mathios Arkangelo, a twenty-eight-year-old Black man from Edmonton, Alberta, Canada was walking down the street, asking for assistance after he stated his car had been stolen. Police arrived on the scene guns drawn as Arkangelo raised his hands. The video shows a great distance between Arkangelo and the police. Arkangelo takes a few steps forwards and is then shot by the police. He falls to the ground. More than two minutes go by before police officers go up to his body, still with guns drawn; they roll him over and handcuff him on the ground. As nine officers stand around, Arkangelo slowly dies before paramedics show up nine minutes later. He later died from the police-inflicted injuries. Anna Odo, Mathios's mother, began a one-woman campaign to get justice for her son and family (Anchan). She joins many other Canadian mothers and families demanding accountability: Mireille Bence, whose son Jean René Junior Olivier was killed by police in Repentigny, Quebec (CTV News); Yvonne Campbell, whose son D'Andre Campbell was shot and killed in his home by police in Brampton, Ontario (The Fifth Estate); and Claudette Korchinski-Beals, whose daughter Regis Korchinski-Paquet died from a fall from a balcony after being alone with police who arrived to undertake a wellness check (Nasser).

Interestingly, much of the movement's growth happened against the backdrop of the COVID-19 pandemic. Staying safe at home was the pandemic's motto. However, in the favelas of Brazil, poor and predominantly Black neighbourhoods, police brutality did not allow residents to obey this rule. In 2020, Black Lives Matter protests erupted in the country after a disastrous police operation killed fourteen-year-old Joao Pedro Mattos Pinto (Freelon). The young Black man was playing with friends in his uncle's house when police officers invaded it, shooting and looking for criminals. The house was hit more than seventy times, and a rifle bullet hit João Pedro in the back. The police then put him in a helicopter allegedly to render aid, but his family members found him dead several hours later in the hospital. In another neighbourhood, just two months later, students were distributing food for those in need when the gunfire scared the eighty people participating in an event. Rodrigo Cerqueira, a nineteen-year-old, was fatally shot (Rouvenat).

Within the few examples shared here, we see similar situations of racial discrimination, murder, imprisonment, and terror occurring in Brazil, Canada, and the US, to name only a few locations. Homicides occupy both race and place. The exposure of Black populations to daily situations of violence indicates an interaction of structural aspects, such as racism, poverty, and gender discrimination, related to socioeconomic, cultural, and ideological causes.

Just as the list of names of unarmed Black folks murdered by the police continues to grow,[2] efforts to end anti-Black violence in all its forms continue to gain steam. Interestingly, and as George Floyd's final words reveal, mothers remain a central touchstone of this movement. Mothers and those who engage in carework are central to the survival of communities, especially during times of struggle and crisis. It is impossible to think of Black men and women of the African diaspora surviving ongoing acts of gratuitous and structural violence without considering the social, cultural, and emotional contribution of Black women and mothers. From resistance to slavery in Brazil, antilynching strategies in the US and struggles to transcend anti-Black genocide in various countries of the African diaspora, it is impossible to deny the importance of the mothering work of Black women in political strategies to guarantee the lives of their loved ones and other people in their communities.

We remember the important role played by Harriet Tubman, who escaped slavery and subsequently rescued nearly seventy enslaved people using the network of antislavery activists and shelters known as the Underground Railroad (Lowry). Viola Desmond, a civil and women's rights activist from Nova Scotia (now featured on Canada's ten-dollar bill) who refused to leave a whites-only section of a cinema, was subsequently charged and spent time in jail for pushing back against blatant racial discrimination. In Brazil, we remember Teresa of Benguela, who became the queen of the Quilombo de Quariterê. Under her leadership, Black and Indigenous communities resisted slavery for two decades (Maceda). Black women in Brazil, Canada, and the United States are denouncing state violence against young Black men and women, who are routinely treated as suspects. Generally, they are also the ones who express the pain of their mourning and cry out for justice for the death of their sons and daughters and the other children of the community, following the legacy of the Black radical tradition (Austin; Robinson).

This structural violence means that Black women are directly affected by the social, economic, and emotional consequences of the violence committed against the Black population. Each life lost cuts deeply into the network of relatives and friends of the murdered, and especially into the lives of mothers, who are often single mothers or the family's main financial providers. This causes enormous suffering, pain, sadness, and despair. Still, these mothers show us their ability to fight against the structures that dismantle their families—that is, trying to guarantee the physical existence of their children and the children of the community.

The mothers of, for example, Trayvon Martin, Michael Brown, Jermaine Carby, and Tamir Rice (to name a few) reveal the strength and resilience of mothers as they demand justice and challenge the power structures that took the lives of their children. We also see this historically. The image of Mamie Till and Emmet Till's open casket funeral in the US and the historic search for justice carried out by Mães de Acari in Brazil come to mind. However, we have also witnessed the day-to-day toll of anti-Black violence. The deaths of Erica Garner (Eric Garner's daughter), Venida Browder (Kalief Browder's mother), the parents of Atatiana Jefferson, and Janaina Soares (Christian Soares's mother) stand as chilling examples and testaments to the concrete effects of this ongoing terror.

The impetus behind this collection began with an interest in exploring the experience of mothering and motherwork[3] as well as the movements and efforts to protect and value Black life. Taking our cue from the work of Patricia Hill Collins,[4] we build on her definition of motherwork as a form of "reproductive labour," which "recognizes that individual survival, empowerment and identity require group survival, empowerment, and identity" (*Black* 199). She goes on to say:

> The term "motherwork" ... soften[s] the existing dichotomies in feminist theorizing about motherhood that posit rigid distinctions between private and public, family and work, the individual and the collective, identity as individual autonomy, identity growing from the collective self-determination of one's group. Racial ethnic women's mothering and work experiences occur at the boundaries demarking these dualities. "Work for the day to come" is motherwork, whether it is on behalf of one's own biological children, or for the children of one's own racial ethnic community, or to preserve the earth for those children who are yet unborn. (*Black* 199)

We sought to be inclusive by incorporating Collins's understanding of othermothers and community mothers:

> Biological mothers, or bloodmothers, are expected to care for children. But African and African-American communities have also recognized that vesting one person with the full responsibility for mothering a child may not be wise or possible. As a result, othermothers—women who assist bloodmothers by sharing mothering responsibilities—traditionally have been central to the institution of Black motherhood. ("Shifting" 179)

She then goes on to say that "Grandmothers, sisters, aunts, or cousins act as othermothers by taking on child-care responsibilities for one another's children" ("Shifting" 179). In this way, we in no way solely prioritize the experiences of biological mothers in this collection. We include in our analysis all mothers—single mothers, queer mothers, trans mothers, disabled mothers, adoptive mothers, to name a few—as well as nonbinary Black folk who do not identify with the gendered label of "mother" but contribute to the important work of caring for families, children, and communities.

As editors, we were also interested in global perspectives that explore historical examinations of the aforementioned topic and contemporary examples rooted in the current political moment. Finally, we hoped to explore visions of the just world that we, and other Black mother/care workers, hope to create for the future.

It is important to note that our work here is, of course, also positioned against the historic judgments hurled against Black mothers. Black feminist scholars have done tremendous work to examine efforts to distance Black women from the ideals of virtue, womanhood, and legitimate motherhood (Spillers; Roberts). Other works have contextualized and historicized problematic and racist conceptualizations of Black motherhood (Berry; Collins; Glenn; Hartman; Roberts). Part of our work here is not only writing against false notions and "controlling images" but "honoring our mothers' sacrifices by self-defined analyses of Black Motherhood" (Collins, "Shfting" 173). This means attempting to centre Black mothers' voices and lived experiences with neither a pathologizing nor idolizing gaze that erases or diminishes the nuances, complexities, and humanity in their experiences.

Personal Reflections and Positionality

Our journey to put together this collection began in 2020. It is not lost on us that four years have passed since we started this endeavour. We are ever so grateful to Andrea O'Reilly and Demeter Press for trusting us to hold this work and for her patience over the years. Looking back, we can boldly say that this book has been a labour of love, frustration, and, at times, even pain. Embedded within these pages are the blood, sweat, and tears of three Black women whose lived experiences exist at the intersections of Blackness, queerness, womanhood, and motherhood. These experiences both informed our desire to facilitate the curation of this body of work and deeply affected our ability and capacity to birth it. Although we hoped to grapple with the themes of Black motherwork during a time of intense political, economic, and social upheaval—a moment that we might say we are still deeply embedded in and currently still navigating—we as editors were also trying to survive the moment. During the last four years, we have not been spared the stressors of familial and job changes, relocation, loss, and the vicissitudes of life in general. Even though this might be the case for most people, we want to publicly acknowledge the impact this has had on our project timelines, our contributors, and the administrative aspect of bringing a project like this to life. At the same time, we want to extend ourselves the grace that Black folks and careworkers are often never afforded. This should particularly be the case when a book of this nature seeks to argue that Black motherhood is a particular experience that becomes compounded by the onslaught of racism, sexism, capitalism, etc., enacted on the Black reproductive body. In addition, within this embodiment of "grace," as we have called it here, it is important that we continue to question and imagine a way of being and working that is rooted in love and care while challenging white supremacist and patriarchal institutional values. This is not to say that this is an easy task and we do not feel the pressures of production, but just as the personal is political, so is the professional and creative. We have to believe that we have the space to breathe into our work and that it will, in a sense, birth itself, when it is ready and the moment is right. With this spirit of grace, gratitude, and love, we offer this work.

Coming into this project, each one of us operates from both shared and unique points of departure—from community organizing in Texas and Sudbury to researching maternal health disparities in the US and other forms of state-sanctioned police violence in the favelas of Brazil. We bring lived experiences of pregnancy loss, navigating health systems, aiding others through pregnancy and birth, and raising Black children in oftentimes hostile environments. As editors, we are deeply rooted and personally connected to this topic.

Haile

I come into this space having spent more than fifteen years researching Black motherhood and, more specifically, maternal and infant disparities in my academic and professional life. I also spent many years organizing with a collective of mothers of colour in Texas, which quite frankly was my entree into this research area. I discovered the collective as a new graduate student with a sixth-month-old in tow alongside another good friend, a fellow mother and graduate student. While collaboratively working to improve reproductive health for birthing folks in Texas through legislative lobbying, doula work and training, and helping to create a prenatal care program for Black and brown birthing people, I learned, most of all, so much about love, relationships, activism, and collective power from these amazing women—many of whom I consider to be family for life. One even served as my midwife during my second pregnancy. I am forever changed and grateful for these experiences. Yet, even with this, I can confidently say the daily labour of carework has had the most pronounced impact on my life over the years. Becoming a mother myself truly transformed me, redirected my life, and expanded my understanding in many ways.

My first child was born in April of 2009. I was a young(ish) twenty-two-year-old, single mother who, during pregnancy, had decided to end my law school career; I had been studying at a highly ranked (top fifteen) law school. Although my experience of navigating Black girlhood in a small Texas town exposed me to several racialized and gendered experiences, it was not until I became a mother that the gravity of my reality and my ability to articulate it fully began to take form. I have written previously about my attempt to advocate for myself and my early attempts to establish autonomy as a young Black woman encountering a potentially hostile healthcare system during pregnancy (Cole). In addition, and as a single parent of, now two, beautiful children, in 2020, my mother had a severe heart attack. I then took on the responsibility as the primary caretaker of a family member in recovery, which later turned into a long-term caretaker of an elderly parent, and a younger sibling trying to find her way. It is important to note this happened amid a global pandemic while executing four cross-country relocations over five years.

Despite being a scholar who has spent my entire career studying the impacts of stress on the Black reproductive body, I often find myself feeling what seems to be the weight of the world on my shoulders and neglecting my health and wellness. I have spent nights holding my children and praying for their safety while watching news clips of burning cars and protests and witnessing the growing rolodex of Black names who have perished at the hands of a hostile state. I have also shed tears for myself wondering how I can continue to juggle numerous balls without dropping them and wondering when, not if, my body, mind, and spirit will push themselves to their limits without respite. In the last few years, I have found myself interestingly preoccupied with death. How can one not when we are constantly surrounded by violence in all its many forms? Moreover, the daily onslaughts and death's ravenous stalking of the Black body—and more potently, the Black mother's proclivity to protect themselves, their children, families, and communities from death's cold grip—are, quite frankly, crushing.

I share this not to begin from a downtrodden perspective but rather to be transparent about the backdrop of this work for me and the very real impacts and experiences of a Black mother navigating the world during this time and in this place. I also share this to highlight the importance of community care. I hope my story and those in this collection will continue to reveal that we are not alone in our struggles. It is also of the utmost importance to me to articulate my belief that Black motherwork and carework are life-sustaining and life-saving endeavors that are not to be taken lightly. Yet this work is not new. Those who participate in carework and motherwork have always done so with the unspoken (and spoken) belief that our lives matter. We see these legacies of love in our foodways, in the times that we share and fellowship together, in the histories of the Granny midwives, in our movements, and in our resilience and continued attempts to survive together. The love, work, and care continue on as a light in the darkness. With this energy and through these legacies, I come to this work.

Luciane

April 10, 2007, was a long day for me. I spent the day in a meeting in the office of Criola, a Black women's organization, in downtown Rio de Janeiro, Brazil. As usual, I met with our partners and community leaders in different neighbourhoods across the city to strategize and evaluate actions regarding improving Black women's health in the peripheries and poor areas of Rio. The meeting ended around 4:00 p.m., and I spent another two hours preparing a report in the office. When I left the organization, I felt a deep sadness and did not want to go straight home. Instead, I went to the nearby street and looked through its shops for a while. On my way to the bus stop, my mother called me and asked if I was staying late at the office, which was customary when we were finalizing projects. "Is everything okay?" "Yes, just checking." My mother was protecting me. When I arrived at my matrilineal family's communal yard, two female cousins were waiting on the sidewalk, and we walked together towards the gate while I told them about the difficult day I had just had. At some point, as we walked into the yard heading to the houses, I saw my mother and two aunts with their heads down and swollen eyes. "What happened?" I asked. "Cosme is dead," a voice let me know. My heartbeat sped up. I went inside his mother's house and saw a devastated woman. Embracing a picture of her son, she was lost in her suffering and sorrow. I knew I could do nothing to help her or myself. I touched her arm, left the house, and started to cry. After the three bullets that had penetrated his back were taken out and he was buried, his parents preferred to stay in silence in sorrow and helped raise his two children. The mothering work I witnessed after this event inspired my doctoral research about the consequences of violence on Black women's lives and their strategies for survival (Rocha).

I have been collaborating with mothers who had children killed by the police and have been fighting for justice for about fourteen years now. From accompanying them in judicial hearings and trials, organizing protests, and editing biographies, I could understand their pedagogies of resistance and the epistemologies of their antagonism with the state. But more than that, we learned to nurture, care, and mother each other. I met these mothers due to their loss and suffering, but in contrast, they taught me about searching for life in abundance, imagining new possibilities, happiness, and love. They also taught me about dreaming the impossible history. Every year, on their deceased children's birthday, they regret not being able to see them aging and wonder what they would be doing. They never forget how old they would be turning and their last times together. My aunt reminded me of when my cousin should have turned forty. Today, he would be a grandfather of two kids if he had seen his kids grow. The impossible history. What would my life be like if I didn't have two miscarriages while we were trying to organize this book? The impossible history. "Is everything okay?" I asked. "Yes, just checking," my mom said.

Shana

The year 2020 was spectacular and life-changing for many across the globe. Between a worldwide pandemic, growing polarization and continued calls for Indigenous sovereignty, in the small northern Ontario town of Sudbury, the demand for racial justice was regaining momentum.

I had been living in this Canadian mining town for thirteen years. I had been separated from my common-law female partner for the last six years, raising out three queerly spawned kids down the block from each other. It was a hopeful time for me, as I was solidifying my work as a public health practitioner and teaching part-time in gender studies. I had also just met a new potential partner online. I was manifesting good things, as I found myself deep within this romantic moment.

I remember the day that George Floyd was killed. As a Black queer woman with three kids, two of whom were currently identifying as boys and one queer girl coming into her own, I immediately acted. I wept, cursed, and raged. I couldn't stop talking about it at work, with my new partner, ex, and kids. It did not take much for me to organize.

A few days later, I connected with my activist networks, and we held a silent grieving session in front of the city's courthouse. It seemed the best place to gather when we were looking for justice. We had done so when demanding reparations for the death of Indigenous twenty-two-year-old, Colten Boushie and supporting the Wet'suwet'en, who were standing against the building of yet another pipeline through their territories.

Protest in this Northern Ontario town was mainly centred around the rights of First Nations, Inuit, Métis, and urban Indigenous folks. I had helped organize multiple rallies (e.g., Take Back the Night, Slut Walk, and Pride) in this city, and we had always known how important it was to centre the voices of Indigenous folks, who were often coleading these events. When George Floyd died, and I once again cried for my three young Black kids, I had hoped that folks would show up for Black people. And indeed, they did.

I have been an activist, academic, and more recently, health system manager for twenty-five years. I found myself advocating for the rights of others back when I was a small child, leading fellow Black community members up the stairs of our national parliament, singing the civil rights song, "We Shall Overcome." I implored my school administrators to listen to the words of fellow racialized students in my 90 per cent white school, who had shared with me examples of the racism they had endured. I walked the streets to Take Back the Night in university, and during my postgraduate years, I joined anti-WTO and antiglobalization protests in Washington, DC and Quebec City. After moving to a new city in 2007, with a fifteen-month-old on my hip and a brand-new community to find, I promptly located Pride organizers and immersed myself in the feminist community. But I had never organized around antiracism specifically (even though, as a women and gender studies professor, intersectionality was always my centre).

Over the next few months, the demands for justice for Black people began. Our city had a tiny Black community; the 2021 census marked just over five thousand Black people in a town of 180,000 (White). However, the growing number of young Black people was evident, and it was not hard to find those who were ready to take action. The call-out (and response) began in earnest: a rally of over two hundred people in our largest park; a sit-in commemorating the Shelbourne Riots, a specific Canadian example of racism; and a bilingual BIPOC Lives Matter mural emblazoned in progress pride colours and bookmarked by two huge dreamcatchers on a downtown street.

I joined a group of twenty-year-old students in the summer of 2020, asking how I could help. Being twenty years their senior, I had experience to share. We formed a board of directors right away and began the process of birthing a movement in a city that was not ready for these types of demands for antiracist action.

It was hard not to look at these brilliant, energized young Black adults and not feel a sense of pride and protection for them. I had my own three Black children I was raising in this town, and I knew what it meant to live as Black (and queer) in these streets. I took on the roles I am used to taking on: doing administrative work, applying for grants, organizing meetings and minutes, and making sure our financials were in check. My connections in the city allowed me to tap into networks for funds, and my previous activist experience helped keep the calm when the police continued to call us at our homes and workplaces. Some of these BLM volunteers were going on to graduate school and wanted my insight on that process. Others were just weary from the ongoing micro (and macro) aggressions and wanted to know how I coped. Was I helping to mother a movement? Perhaps. But I know that motherwork always shows up in activist circles for Black women, and I saw this very clearly in the way we came together during that time.

When the opportunity to support this edited collection arrived, it made sense to me as someone who had previous work focussed on mothering in alternative spaces and research that investigated the historical emergence of Girl Guiding in the Caribbean (Calixte). I wanted to understand how those engaging in motherwork saw this about the Black Lives Matter movement. It is not surprising that the movements in the US, Toronto, and Sudbury were started by Black queer women, many of whom were mothers. This needs to be honoured as integral to the movement for Black lives: the clear link between the radical work done as mothers, and specifically as Black mothers, and this new civil rights movement, ignited by the violent murder of a Black man who cried for his mother.

This book has been a labour of love, as we negotiated a pandemic, changing family structures and work orientations, and various losses. We came together as strangers who knew that a story existed out there on this subject and that our personal experiences as caretakers of Black knowledge and struggle would be mirrored in the words of colleagues out there who had something to say about this ongoing work for racial justice. The activism, artistry, or, as my fellow Black Lives Matter crew would say, "artivism" of this moment need to be heard and understood. We hope this is felt as you move through the pages of this collection.

Book Organization

The resulting pages of this work include traditional academic research and writing as well as poetry, creative nonfiction, art, and photography. The collection is structured thematically into four sections. The first section deals with the theme of education, both formal and informal—that is, the lessons Black mothers impart to their children to ensure their survival. For the contributors in this section, education can range from encouraging Black children to pursue education for access and social mobility or learning preparedness by observing the seemingly bottomless articles in your grandmother's purse.

Section two explores various manifestations of motherwork via essay, poetry, and photography. This includes both the joys and challenges of navigating motherhood in the era of Black Lives Matter and parallel health pandemics as well as the important role of othermothers, such as aunties and extended family. Most importantly, these pieces embody the themes of lasting love and resilience so critical to Black motherwork.

The third section of the collection deals with experiences of and reactions to incidences of trauma and ongoing violence. With Haile's photograph titled *Almost Human*, the chapter begins by calling into question the humanity or perceived (in)humanity of Black bodies and in particular Black youth. The other pieces in this section chronicle various manifestations of violence as experienced by Black mothers, families, and communities. A slightly controversial inclusion in this section examines the role of spanking and corporal punishment within Black families. Our decision to include this piece relates to a viral moment from 2015 when a Baltimore mother was captured on video physically striking her son for rioting during a protest and stating that she did not want him to "end up like Freddie Gray," a Black man in Baltimore who was arrested, sustained injuries, and later died while in custody (CBS News). The chapter explores the contentious dialogue of discipline as an attempt to protect Black children amid mothers' fears of state violence.

Finally, the last section includes contributions that explore the themes of resistance and hope. Overall, our desire here is simple: to create a space for Black folks engaged in motherwork of various forms to share their stories and to reveal, even if only a bit, the small pieces of patchwork that create the fabric and legacies of love, care, and survival in our communities.

Endnotes

1. For more on the radical traditions of Black organizing across Canada, see Mullings et al.; Tomlinson; Pasternak et al.
2. In 2024, the Ontario Human Rights Commission released a report on anti-Black racism in Toronto's police force.
3. See Collins, Patricia Hill. *Black feminist thought*. Vol. 11. New York. Routledge, 2000.
4. See Collins, Patricia Hill. "Shifting the Center: Race, Class, and Feminist Theorizing about Motherhood" in *American Families: A Multicultural Reader.* Coontz, Stephanie, Maya Parson, and Gabrielle Raley, eds. Psychology Press, 1999.

Works Cited

Anchan, Mrinali. "Family of Mathios Arkangelo and Allies Demand Justice Outside EPS Stations." *CBC News*, 1 Aug. 2024, https://www.cbc.ca/news/canada/edmonton/family-of-mathios-arkangelo-and-allies-demand-justice-outside-eps-stations-1.7281893. Accessed 22 Dec. 2024.

Austin, David. "All Roads Led to Montreal: Black Power, the Caribbean, and the Black Radical Tradition in Canada." *The Journal of African American History*, vol. 92, no. 4, 2007, pp. 516–39.

Calixte, Shana L. "Baby, Belly, Boundaries: The Effect of Pregnancy on Research Relationships." *Maternal Geographies: Mothering in and out of place.* Edited by Jennifer L. Johnson and Krista Johnston. Demeter Press, 2019, pp. 135–48.

Calixte, Shana L. "Beyond 'Us' Versus 'Them': Transnationalizing Girlhood Studies. *Difficult Dialogues about Twenty-First-Century Girls.* Edited by Donna Marie Johnson and Alice E. Ginsberg. Suny Press, 2015, pp. 145–79.

CBS News. "Baltimore Mom Who Smacked Son during Riots: 'I Don't Want Him to Be a Freddie Gray.'" CBS News, 28 Apr. 2015, https://www.cbsnews.com/news/baltimore-mother-toya-graham-on-why-she-smacked-son-i-dont-want-him-to-be-a-freddie-gray/. Accessed 22 Dec. 2024.

Cole, Haile Eshe. "A Love Letter to My Daughter: Love as a Political Act." *Birthing Justice*. Edited by Julie Chinyere Oparah and Alicia Bonaparte. Routledge, 2023, pp. 185–90.

Collins, Patricia Hill. *Black Feminist Thought*. Routledge, 2000.

Collins, Patricia Hill. "Shifting the Center: Race, Class, and Feminist Theorizing about Motherhood." *American Families: A Multicultural Reader*. Edited by Stephanie Coontz. Psychology Press, 1999, pp. 173–87.

CTV News. "Mother of Black Man Killed by Repentigny Police Seeks $430,000 from City." CTV News, 28 Feb. 2023, https://montreal.ctvnews.ca/articles-by-amy-luft/mother-of-black-man-killed-by-repentigny-police-seeks-430-000-from-city-1.6292988 Accessed 22 Dec. 2024.

Freelon, Kiratiana. "How the Police Killing of a Black Brazilian Teen Sparked a Movement." *Yes Movement*, 27 Aug. 2020, https://www.yesmagazine.org/social-justice/2020/08/27/brazil-movement-for-black-lives. Accessed 22 Dec. 2024.

Lowry, Beverly. *Harriet Tubman: Imagining a Life*. Anchor Books, 2008.

Maceda, Luane. "4 aprendizados fundamentais para lideranças a partir do legado de Tereza de Benguela." *Portal Geledés*, 3 Aug. 2023, https://www.geledes.org.br/4-aprendizados-fundamentais-para-lideran-cas-a-partir-do-legado-de tereza-de-benguela/. Accessed 22 Dec. 2024.

Mullings, Delores V., et al. "Canada the Great White North Where Anti-Black Racism Thrives: Kicking Down the Doors and Exposing the Realities." *Phylon*, vol. 53, no. 1, 2016, pp. 20–41. JSTOR, http://www.jstor.org/stable/phylon1960.53.1.20 Accessed 10 Nov. 2024.

Nasser, Shanifa. "Family of Regis Korchinski-Paquet Puts Interview with Police watchdog on Hold after Leak by 'Sources.'" *CBC News*, 3 June 2020, https://www.cbc.ca/news/canada/toronto/regis-korchins-ki-paquet-toronto-1.5596811. Accessed 22 Dec. 2024.

Ontario Human Rights Commission. *From Impact to Action: Final Report into Anti-Black Racism by the Toronto Police Service*. OHRC, https://www3.ohrc.on.ca/en/impact-action-final-report-anti-black-racism-toronto-police-service. Accessed 22 Dec. 2024.

Pasternak, Shiri, et al., editors. *Disarm, Defund, Dismantle: Police Abolition in Canada*. Between the Lines, 2022.

Robinson, Cedric. *Black Marxism: The Making of the Black Radical Tradition*. University of North Carolina Press, 2000.

Rocha, Luciane. "Black Mothers' Experiences of Violence in Rio de Janeiro." *Cultural Dynamics*, vol. 24, no. 1, 2012, pp. 59–74.

Rocha, Luciane. Maternidad indignada: reflexiones sobre el activismo de las madres negras. *ANTHROPOLOGICA/AÑO XXXVI*, no. 41, 2018, pp. 35–56.

Rouvenat, Fernanda. "Shooting Interrupts Distribution of Basic Food Baskets in Providência; 19-Year-Old Dies in the Action." *Yes Magazine*, 5 May 2020, https://g1.globo.com/rj/rio-de-janeiro/noticia/2020/05/22/tiroteio-interrompe-distribuicao-de-cestas-basicas-na-providencia-jovem-de-19-anos-morre-na-acao.ghtml. Accessed 22 Dec. 2024.

The Fifth Estate. "Shot by Police, D'Andre Campbell's Family Wants Officers Charged." *YouTube*, 7 June 2020, https://www.youtube.com/watch?v=x9YVDCyo0X8&ab_channel=TheFifthEstate. Accessed 22 Dec. 2024.

White, Erik. "A New Face Entirely": Northern Ontario's Growing Black Community Looks to the Future during History Month." *CBC News*, 21 Feb. 2023, https://www.cbc.ca/news/canada/sudbury/black-community-northern-ontario-1.6747837. Accessed 22 Dec. 2024.

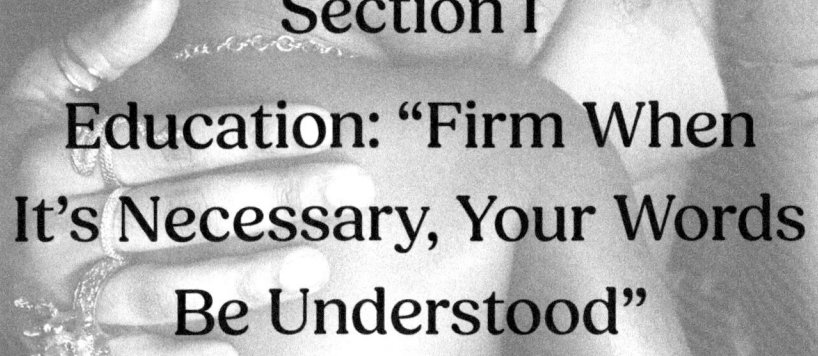

Section I
Education: "Firm When It's Necessary, Your Words Be Understood"

1.

Mother and Child

Devynity

Artist's Statement

Devynity is a Black woman writer and visual artist from Queens, NY, whose work reflects her heritage and upbringing. Devynity's written and visual work are intertwined, both mediums offering a space to examine contemporary themes within the Black experience to illuminate the nuanced stories of struggle, resilience, love, and transformation that shape her communities and the diaspora at large. Her practice explores how race, gender, and history collide and collude to impact personal and collective identity. At the heart of her words is a commitment to truth-telling—honouring the past, engaging with the present and imagining a future grounded in authenticity and empowerment, always endeavouring to contribute to a broader dialogue about representation and the ongoing journey toward justice and equity.

2.

Freedom Choices: How Black Mothers Living in the Jim Crow Era Protected Their Children from Anti-Black Racism and Prepared Them for Success

LaShawnDa Pittman, Alana Lim, Ayan Mohamed, Mia Schuman, Rachel Vulk, and Rina Yan

This chapter examines how Black mothers devised strategies of resistance to prepare their children for success and protect them from anti-Black racism during the Jim Crow era (1881–1964) from a Black feminist perspective, which calls for an interpretation of Black women's experiences and ideas by those who participate in them (Collins 15). We rely on Black women's perspectives to understand how interlocking systems of oppression shaped their mothering experiences during the Jim Crow era's de facto and de jure racism, which created a neoslavery system in which American culture, societal norms, laws, and public policies were based on rigid racial hierarchies that placed Black people at the very bottom of a caste system that used "powerful infrastructure" to hold "each group in its place" (Wilkerson 19). Black feminist standpoint theory clarifies a particular standpoint of and for Black women. A Black women's standpoint—"those experiences and ideas shared by African American women that provide a unique angle of vision on self, community, and society" (Collins 22)—creates specialized knowledge based on their ways of knowing the world. From this perspective, the history of Black women is embedded in their lived experiences. Black women's experiences are therefore crucial to the construction of theory and knowledge production about Black mothering. Thus, we ask what are Black women's childrearing experiences from their perspectives? How did they make sense of and respond to their lack of rights and adequate resources stemming from their experiences of Jim Crow-era racism?

We also consider Black mothering from a reproductive justice perspective, which asserts women's personal right to control their body, have children under the conditions that they choose, and parent those children in stable communities (SisterSong). In 1994, Black women created the reproductive justice framework to provide "a powerful tool for exploring issues of racial, economic, and social inequality by building on Black feminist theory and applying those insights to reproductive politics" (Ross et al. 11). The reproductive justice framework is rooted in analyzing power systems and intersecting oppressions and centering the marginalized. It strayed from historically rigid representations of women's rights and reproductive politics led by white, middle-class groups on both sides of the abortion debate. Beyond abortion, reproductive justice recognizes "women of color and other marginalized women also often have difficulty accessing: contraception, comprehensive sex education, STI prevention and care, alternative birth options, adequate prenatal and pregnancy care, domestic violence assistance, adequate wages to support our families, safe homes, and so much more" (SisterSong). In this chapter, we explore how Jim Crow-era racism undermined Black women's right to parent their children in safe and healthy environments. We explore how anti-Black racism, white supremacy, and patriarchy hindered Black women's realization of this aspect of reproductive justice, and what strategies of resistance they devised in response.

Although several factors impeded Black mothers' right to parent the children they have in safe and healthy environments—including their unequal access to resources and societal institutions (e.g., education, healthcare, employment, and housing)—we focus on how Black mothers responded to their children's exposure to anti-Black racism and unequal access to quality education. The racial hostility and violence that Black people were subjected to during the Jim Crow era made ensuring their children's safety foremost in Black mothers' minds. Although many mothers may feel compelled to protect their children, not all mothers must protect them from anti-Black racism. Black mothers have had to devise strategies to protect their children from systemic racism in all of its manifestations, including racialized violence. The centrality and significance of this protective function to Black mothering are not new. However, every generation of Black mothers must devise adapted strategies of resistance to confront how anti-Black racism is codified into laws and policies and becomes naturalized and normalized in the era they must parent their children. In this chapter, we describe the form and tenor of anti-Black racism during the Jim Crow era. Moreover, we show that Black mothers did so by utilizing informal education—which we define as a protective strategy used to teach children how to safely navigate and negotiate racial hostility and violence—to teach their children when to deploy restraint and resistance and how to navigate white space. Finally, we show that Black mothers relied on both informal and formal education to ensure their children's safety and success.

Racism, poverty, and exposure to anti-Black racism forced Black mothers to use education as the primary site to enlarge their children's opportunities and prepare them for success. Women in this study unanimously agreed that education was central to their children's ability to achieve success in adulthood, which is consistent with previous research that shows that regardless of their socioeconomic status, Black people highly value education (Herelle; Diamond and Gomez). We discuss the structural barriers that cultivated an apartheid education for Black children, making it difficult for their mothers to ensure that they received an equal education. We argue that in the face of apartheid education, Black mothers strategized to provide their children choices in the present that would give them more freedom and opportunities in the future. We refer to this mothering practice as the cultivation of "freedom choices". Freedom choices seek to minimize hindrances and restraints that shape the choices available to Black families and expand their available options. Although both "freedom choices" and "freedom of choice" stress that individuals have options and agency, they differ in two important ways. First, with freedom choices there is no assumption of freedom or the freedom to choose. During the Jim Crow era, laws were deliberately designed to restrict the rights of African Americans, including the rights to vote, work, and receive an education. In contrast, freedom of choice implies freedom and the freedom to choose. Second, freedom of choice implies access to the breadth and depth of opportunities available to an individual in the environment they inhabit. Their social context significantly constrains Black people's freedom of choice. Freedom choices acknowledge these constraints as Black mothers push to enlarge the boundaries of their children's choices by ensuring they can access, among other things, an education. Third, freedom of choice centres on individual decision-making. In contrast, freedom choices focus on the choices available to those within a group—in this case, the choices available to Black people.

Jim Crow and Black Mothering

When slavery ended, Black codes and Jim Crow laws sought to institute a system as close to slavery as the newly passed thirteenth, fourteenth, and fifteenth amendments would allow (Dunaway; Gates). Jim Crow policies reclaimed and exploited Black labour through threats of actual acts of violence and incarceration, "the cultivation of the fear of such violence," and incarceration, thereby trapping the majority of African Americans in domestic, personal service, and agricultural work for nearly a century (Gates 127). Strict labour laws kept Black workers under the economic and social control of white landowners (Dunaway; Gates; Jones). Racial discrimination combined with racial violence by law enforcement and white vigilantes shut African Americans out of most segments of the labour market, forcing most Black people to live in poverty (Althoff and Reichardt; Dunaway; Gates; Jones).

In her work on the meaning of mothering among Black women, sociology professor Patricia Hill Collins notes, "Black mothers also pay the cost of giving up their own dreams of achieving full creative ability. Because many spend so much time feeding the physical needs of their children" (136). While this is true of many mothers, Black women's involvement in the labour market has made their experiences different from those of other women. Black mothers are more likely than all other women to work outside of the home, to be their family's primary breadwinner, and to experience significant racial wage disparities (Pittman).

Historically, Black women have participated in the labour force at higher rates than white women. They enter the labour market younger, continue working after marriage, and stay in the workforce longer (Jones). Economics professor Claudia Goldin found that "labor force participation for white women more than doubled between 1890 and 1960, increasing from 16.3 percent to 33.7 percent, while that for non-white women remained almost constant (39.7 percent to 41.7 percent)" (87). So, while white women doubled their labour market participation rates from around the beginning to the end of the Jim Crow era, Black women were already abundantly represented. These racial differences have been driven by Black men's lower earnings and higher unemployment rates relative to white men, Black peoples' lower non-labour income (e.g., social security and other transfer payments associated with aging, disability, and economic hardship), a higher prevalence of female-headed households among Black people, and distinct social norms within Black and white communities (Goldin). Census data beginning in 1870 has revealed racial differences in labor market participation to exist even when women share characteristics—"the presence of preschool children, a woman's education and training, the level of non-labor income, and the husband's unemployment experience" (Goldin 89).

During the Jim Crow era, white women worked in the clerical, sales, and retail sectors and in professional and technical occupations. They also worked as operators in industry/manufacturing and as proprietors and managers (Maloney). Racism prohibited Black women from working in these occupations. Instead, Black women found work as domestics, laundresses, and farm workers. They also earned an income by taking in boarders, working as hairstylists, midwives, and herbalists and selling homegrown vegetables, eggs, and livestock. Some Black women owned small businesses and worked as skilled laborers and artisans. Black women who obtained more education worked as teachers, nurses, doctors, dentists, and journalists. In addition to their underrepresentation in higher paying occupations, Black women's lower wages for the same work also contributed to their earning disparities.

Black women's annual earnings have been and continue to be significantly lower than white women's: In 1939, it was $331.32 compared to $771.69; in 1949, it was $992.35 compared to $1781.96; in 1959, it was $1412.16 compared to $2371.80; and in 1969, it was $3205.12 compared to $3786.45 (Maloney). Black women's wage penalty[1] affects Black families, since Black mothers are more likely to be breadwinners in their families. Between 1880 and 1960, African Americans had higher rates of single-parent households compared to whites: 11.7 percent compared to 8.2 percent in 1880, and 9.9 percent compared to 5.5 percent in 1960 for Black and white families, respectively (Ruggles).

Black mothers' experiences have also been distinct from other mothers because they face significant racial disparities in maternal and infant mortality rates. Poverty and racism impeded Black women's ability to care for their children before, during, and after childbirth. Racism has been shown to significantly contribute to persistent racial disparities in infant and maternal mortality and morbidity (Alson et al.). Even when controlling for the social conditions of women's lives, such as their socioeconomic status, employment status, education level, geographic location, and the safety and environmental health of their community, Black women's exposure to racism (e.g., racism-related stress and weathering (early health deterioration, as measured across biological indicators of repeated exposure and adaptation to stressors) contributes to their higher rates of maternal and infant mortality and morbidity (e.g., preterm birth, low birth weight) compared with other women (Dominguez; Geronimus et al.). Before the passage of Title V of the Social Security Act (1935), Black women's maternal mortality rates were nearly double that of white women. Similarly, in 1916, the infant mortality rate for Black infants was 87 percent higher than the rate for white infants. In 1920, the Black infant mortality rate was 43 percent higher than the white infant mortality rate. By 2017, the Black infant mortality rate was 122 percent higher than the white infant mortality. So, while white mothers and infants have experienced marked declines in their mortality rates, the same has not been true of Black mothers and infants (Singh and Yu 21).

Regardless of their socioeconomic status, geography, and the period they live in, Black mothers must contend with the impact of racialized violence on their children's lives. During the Jim Crow era, Black mothers had to devise strategies to protect their sons from the "violence of segregation and Jim Crow culture—through lynching, police brutality, economic terrorism, and a vastly unequal justice system" (Simmons 2). The Tuskegee Institute in Alabama documented more than 4,700 lynchings between 1882 and 1964 (Bailey and Tolnay). Black mothers had to strategize to protect their daughters from the violence enacted on Black girls, including sexual violence, and the physical and emotional violence Black girls encountered as they confronted "For Whites Only" signs, faced racist narratives of Black femininity, and negotiated the politics of respectability about what a proper girl should be.

Racial disparities in maternal and infant mortality rates and earnings persist. Between 1935 and 2015, the risk of maternal mortality remained three to four times higher among Black women than white women, as white women experienced a more rapid decline in maternal mortality than Black women (Singh and Yu). Black women as a group have laboured more intensively than white women,[2] yet they earn less, despite wage gains during the 1940s and 1960s.[3] Studies consistently find that even when considering and controlling for differences in productivity, education, industry, and occupation, substantial differences in the racial wage gap across genders persist (Paul et al.; Goldin). Labour force participation rates are also highest for Black mothers. In 2020, 76 percent of Black mothers were in the labor force, compared with 71.3 percent of white mothers, 62.8 percent of Chicana/Latina mothers, and 64.3 percent of Asian mothers. Eighty percent of Black mothers are the breadwinners in their families (Roux). Black mothering also continues to be shaped by punitive and disciplinary forms of governance, as Black children experience disproportionate and more severe punishment from school authorities, law enforcement, and the criminal justice system (Elliott and Reid).

Data and Methods

We analyzed oral histories from Duke University's Behind the Veil Oral History Project and Harvard University's Black Women's Oral History Project. The Behind the Veil Oral History Project was undertaken by Duke University's Center for Documentary Studies from 1993 to 1995. Funded by the National Endowment for the Humanities, the project's primary purpose was to record and preserve the living memory of African American life during the age of legal segregation in the American South from the 1890s to the 1950s. Over three summers, teams of researchers conducted oral history interviews with more than one thousand elderly Black Southerners who remembered and lived through that period of legal segregation. It is the largest single collection of Jim Crow oral histories, with 1,260 interviews in the collection. We analyzed one-hundred thirty-eight interviews with female interviewees (in some cases male interviewees and additional female interviewees were also present). We also analyzed the seventy-two interviews conducted with the women interviewed for the Black Women Oral History Project. These women who lived through the Jim Crow era were interviewed between 1976 and 1981. With support from the Schlesinger Library, the project recorded a cross-section of women who had made significant contributions to American society during the first half of the twentieth century.

We used Dedoose cloud-based software to code the interviews for core themes related to mothering and childhood experiences, experiences of racism and sexism, socioeconomic experiences, access to medical care, and protective factors. We used grounded theory, which involves constructing hypotheses and theories by collecting and analyzing data, to identify and make sense of the themes that emerged as significant to the study population (Strauss and Corbin). Through this data analysis, our concept of freedom choices, which contributes to our understanding of Black mothering practices and Black feminist perspectives on mothering, emerged. Coding was cross-checked with all authors to ensure reliability. We worked iteratively between interview data and secondary sources.

Protecting Their Children from Anti-Black Racism

> If you don't raise a boy right, he won't last long. You know what I'm talking about. They kill him. ... And I don't mean cow him down, but you need to instruct them that they treat everybody right.
> —Arthur Clayborn

In general, mothering involves raising children right by imparting lessons and engaging in practices that instill morality, meaning that they know right from wrong and do the right thing. But as Arthur Clayton's comment makes plain, Black mothers must teach their children the right actions and behaviours to keep them alive amid anti-Black racism that follows their children's Black bodies everywhere in the United States (US). What does it mean to raise one's children right if they are Black children coming of age during legalized segregation? For the mothers in this study and their families, it meant:(1) teaching children restraint, resistance, and when to deploy them; and (2) negotiating space, including understanding under what conditions it is safe or unsafe to take up more or less space.

Practising Restraint and Resistance

When Black mothers taught their children, explicitly or implicitly, to practice restraint, they taught them to follow the rules, even if they were not fair. They taught them not to outwardly express their real emotions or feelings about the impact that anti-Black racism had on them. Oral history interviewees' stories revealed how what they had been taught about how to deal with anti-Black racism kicked in when confronted with its various forms. Even if they did not obey what they had been taught, what they learned still surfaced. For instance, Alice Dunnigan (b. 1906), born and raised in Russellville, Kentucky, was taught by her mother to practice restraint in the face of anti-Black racism. Yet she resisted:

> There has always been a racial problem ... a situation I encountered as a young child, about ten years old or so....I would head straight ... into the "White ladies" restroom. My mother opposed this action. Oh, she would get so mad with me, ordering me to stay out of the "White folks" toilet. "Them white folks gonna get you in there some day, and beat you half to death, and there's nothing I can do about it."

As Alice recalled the incident, she made explicit Black mothers' concerns about their children's safety in an environment plagued by racialized violence—not to mention, the lack of recourse Black families had should something happen to their children. Alice's resistance to racialized violence followed her into her adulthood. She became a teacher at the only school for Black students in the county where she lived. She described an incident in which she had been charged with taking a group of her students to take a "final year examination": "Their greatest problem was the availability of a usable rest room. They would come to me and ask, 'Miss Alice, where can we go to the john?' 'Go in there where the white children are going,' I would advise. 'But that says "White ladies" and we are afraid to go in there.' So, I would have to escort each one of them in, whenever they had to go."

Elizabeth Pointer (b. 1927) was born and raised in Tuskegee, Alabama. She learned to practise restraint in the face of a common form of racial violence faced by Black children, racial violence at the hands of white children riding school buses.

> We could not ride the buses although we were paying taxes. But we couldn't ride those buses nothing rode the bus but the whites. And they would ride and throw trash, throw rocks and everything at us on the road and hoop and holler, "n***** n***** n*****" all up and down the road. We weren't allowed to say one word to 'em or not throw back nothing, 'cause you threw back at 'em you was going to jail.

In contrast, Bernice Magruder White (b. 1927) and her sisters exemplified resistance to this form of racial violence:

> But I can remember, when we were in Sunflower County around the Sunflower River, we did get to fighting with a group. We were walking, and every day when the bus came along—it was a narrow road. We had to walk about three miles to this school, and the place was called Kennelock [phonetic].... So, one day we happened to be along when they were putting out about three white students... And so, when they got out of the bus, some words were passed. I don't remember. And one threw—they had these big hard balls of mud ... threw it at us, and we fought. They went running home. They didn't have far to go, but we had about two miles to go. We ran all the way. We didn't tell our parents. We were frightened for about the rest of the remainder of the school, and I think they were frightened, too, because we never had that problem anymore. So, we settled that.

Bernice, who was born in a rural part of Washington County, Mississippi, shared that she and her sisters knew that they could not tell their parents about their response to the racial violence they experienced by white children. She provided insight into how she and most Black children were taught to practise restraint in the face of racial violence and other forms of anti-Black racism. Similarly, Ferdie Walker (b. 1928), born and raised in Fort Worth, Texas, recounted an experience of not filling in the seats at the back:

> And the bus driver got up and came back to tell me that I had to move out of that seat because I had to go all the way back to the back. And it made me so angry. Now I wasn't really a rebellious kid. I followed the rules. I never got in any trouble, but that day, I was just mad. So, I got up and I did not go to the back of the bus

I just stood in the stairwell that you had to walk out of to get off the bus. And he was determined that he was going to make me go and sit down. I was determined I wasn't going to do it. So, I just stood there. And he finally said, "Well, I'm going to have to go get a policeman." And so, I just stood there. And I knew that if my mother knew that I had acted out, that's what it was called, she would really be very upset with me. But I just stood there and when the bus stopped, I just got off and I walked home. I just didn't want to do what he said do. And that's about the most rebellious that I was.

Ferdie balanced the restraint her mother taught her with her own quiet resistance to combat the degradation she experienced when asked to move to the back of the bus. She didn't "act out" but she also didn't comply. While Bernice and Ferdie were taught by their mothers to exercise restraint in the face of anti-Black racism, Abna Lancaster (b. 1907), born and raised in Salisbury, North Carolina, learned indirect and direct resistance from her mother:

I was told to hold my head up and walk with dignity anywhere. However, I knew that water fountains, there was white water and there was colored water, and I would have to drink at the colored water fountain. So, my mother didn't permit us to drink water at any of the fountains. "You don't have to drink that water. Come home. We've got water at home." ... But there were certain things that we just did not accept. For instance, my mother would not buy things from a store in which they called her by her first name. And that was a rather usual thing, because the clerks would say, "Well no, I hope you're satisfied, Mary." Or, "How you doing, Sally?" Something of that kind. But my mother would tell them that she was honorably married, and they would either call her Mrs. Aggrey or would not say anything at all.

Other oral history interviewees shared that they or their parents also refused to shop at stores that forbade Black people from trying on clothes.

Negotiating Space

Negotiating space was about how much or how little space to take up in public and in interactions with whites, including when to move out of the way, where to stand or sit, and enter or exit. Ann Pointer recalled how she was taught to move out of the way when whites passed.

> I had not told [my children] about the oppression, how bitter I had been as a child. I felt like I wasn't nothing ... you coming down the street like this and you meeting a white person coming this way, I don't care if you could be on the sidewalk and he be'd on there but if he and his wife are walking together on there, you going to have to step down in the gutter and let them pass. You walk right up to 'em and they'd tell the sheriff and you'd go to jail.

Negotiating space was also about learning the significance of geography and place—specifically, learning what parts of town, what businesses, and what individuals to avoid and which ones were safe. For example, Ira Lee Jones, born and raised in East Lake, Alabama, recalled how she learned from her mother to avoid a particular nearby neighbourhood because it was known for its high concentration of Ku Klux Klan membership and activity. To earn extra money, Ira's mother went to sit with an elderly white man in the neighbourhood. When he asked her to retrieve a belt from his bedroom, Ira's mother expected him to put it on. Instead, he "just sat up there and started doing this [smacking sound] with the belt and said this was the way I used to whip n*****." Her mother never went back. After that, Ira and her brother were taught to avoid this area. "I don't think we went to 68th Street. Klu Klux Klan and all of those folks lived in that area." Ira continued:

> I don't ever remember them [parents] telling us anything but watch where you go, just be careful where you go 'cause by the time we got in high school my brother had learned to drive. She'd [mother] tell us don't go in certain parts of town, and to be sure what time we were supposed to be back home that we got there. Don't mess around come straight home. When we go to dances at the Civic Center and uh 'cause they would give dances just for Blacks or give dances just for whites.... And they would tell us be sure you get back home ... don't go nowhere else 'cause I want to know where you are, that you're safe. It wasn't that we would get

into anything, there were people …. who even lost their lives and nobody knows today how … just riding along and somebody decided I don't want to see them n***** riding or walking or and whatever, and they'd be gone.

Some mothers tried to shrink the space their children had to roam as much as possible. Arnette and William Earl Davis's brother was murdered by whites in Mississippi for dating a Black girl who was also secretly dating a white man. He was murdered on his twentieth birthday. William Earl described what happened:

> But you know back during that time, you know, Black girls were, you know sneaking out and courting white men. And the same Black girls was courting, the black girls was courting the black guys. But, you know, if the white guy find out about it, you know, they want to use brutality. And that's what happened to my brother, you know … about 4:00, 4:30 that morning I guess some by-pass was going home and saw his body like laying there in the middle of the highway. They busted his skull open, had, used some type of ax or hatchet or something, because half of his skull was found some seven miles away from his main body. It wadn't [sic] only just to bruise on one. Seemed like they punched him in the side with a tire iron. I guess they had to tie his hands or something cause he was very strong.

After their brother was murdered in 1962, Arnette and William Earl Davis's mother became very protective of her remaining six sons and one daughter.

> Arnette Davis: Due to that my mother, like if I go out I always have to be back in by 8:00 o'clock. I did that until I left home that following, the beginning of the winter, you know, the second quarter of the Mississippi Valley State. That was during the time that Dallas State was on the quarter system. So I enrolled in Valley the second quarter after we gathered crops. So I didn't come home no more about two or three times during that whole school term due to the fact that if I come home, you know, I'd be very protected.
>
> William Earl Davis: Very protected. Very sheltered.

Arnette Davis: My mama, she didn't want me to go no place.

William Earl Davis: You could not participate in the sports, special events. Things like that.

William and Arnette's mother knew that their family had no legal recourse to pursue justice for her son. Arnette stated, "You couldn't get any help." So, she controlled to what degree she could, the amount of space her children had to negotiate.

Global gender studies professor Lakisha Michelle Simmons brings attention to how space determined the kinds of physical and verbal assaults and insults that Black girls navigated on Jim Crow streets: "On some city streets black girls might routinely walk by a cacophony of catcalls; on other streets they might have to withstand touching from whites or other physical insults; and ...on some streets black girls faced insults from white children" (58). Bernice Magruder White exemplified how, during segregation, Black mothers tried to protect their daughters from the geography of insults that assailed them, but to no avail. Black girls were most vulnerable outside in the world. Bernice, the mother of three, described an incident where she could not protect the female students she taught while travelling with them to a YMCA meeting:

> I was taking some girls to Laurel, Mississippi to a meeting. It was something like a YMCA meeting, but it was through the high school, and in high school they call it Hi-Y. It was four girls in the car, and this was during the time that they had what they called the sit-ins and marches and freedom riders, as some of them called them. Three of my girls were real light-skinned. One was dark-skinned ... and then I was what you called brown skinned. I got stopped outside of Laurel about one mile, and, of course, we were accused of everything. We were called all kind of slutty names. Sixteen, fifteen, and sixteen-year-old girls, and I'm their teacher ... and he cited me for reckless driving and insulting him. Nobody said a word to him. But what had happened, one of the girls had great big eyes, and they were just kind of this wide around. And so when he came to the door, I let the window down. He reached his hand in and unlocked the door, and then he reached his hand around and unlocked the back door and opened it. He did that, with his hands right here. Oh, that was frightening.

He didn't use any profane, but he used a lot of slut-like, the names he called us. It's embarrassing. It was the worst feeling I ever had.

So I went on to the judge.... I had to pay the fine, which took all the money we had, and that hurt me more than him to belittle me and call me all these names and I couldn't say anything about it, and call these girls all these names and I couldn't say anything about it. We didn't have nothing. He had his gun, he had his night stick, and he told us what he ought to do to us, take us out and beat us all up.

Navigating an Apartheid Education

Africana studies professor Noliwe Rooks defines apartheid education as education that occurs when groups that are not themselves poor or of colour control education curricula and forms offered only to Black people and the poor (50). Rooks maintains, "Skin color and class determined the type of education a student was seen as worthy of acquiring" (50). As a result, Black children were largely relegated to Black-only schools and seldom attended schools frequented by children who were of means (50). The legacy of this early period of education during the Jim Crow era is still with us today.

Immediately following Reconstruction (1868–1877), which made federal funds available for schools, teachers, and school buildings, Southern legislatures "moved aggressively throughout the South to dismantle the political and educational progress Black communities had made" (Rooks 52). Although school segregation was already a fact of life throughout the South, the states where oral history interviewees resided codified this fact of life into law. After wresting control back from Black elected officials, state and local governments immediately passed laws making an integrated education a violation of the law. For example, in 1878, Mississippi lawmakers wrote it into state law by requiring "the schools in each county shall be so arranged as to offer ample free school facilities to all educable youths in that county but white and colored children shall not be taught in the same school-house, but in separate school-houses" (Southern Poverty Leadership Council). Other Southern states followed suit and passed similar legislation.

Rooks identifies how state and local governments "also used their legislative authority to institute policies forbidding the use of 'white tax dollars' to educate Black students. Some states went so far as to require Black people to pay a double tax if they wanted their children educated—one to educate white schoolchildren, and another for the education of their own" (52). In 1890, Mississippi adopted a new constitution that reinforced racially segregated schools and created a new school funding mechanism that allowed wealthy, white school districts to levy taxes for education revenue far above the taxes generated in poor, largely Black districts (Southern Poverty Leadership Council). In the decade before the US Supreme Court declared segregated schools unconstitutional in Brown v. Board of Education (1954), white Mississippians began to recognize that ensuring Black schools were equal to white schools may be the best way to fend off lawsuits that could end segregation. A 1952 state report, however, showed vast disparities between Black and white schools; a Delta district, for example, spent $464.49 per white student but only $13.71 per Black student (Southern Poverty Leadership Council 2017). Similarly, in 1930, Alabama spent $37 on each white child and only $7 on each Black child (Irons).

The magnitude of the educational disparities experienced by Black children is also evident in Black teachers' salaries. In 1891, in one predominantly Black county in Alabama, the total budget for teachers' salaries was $6,545, the same amount they spent per student at white schools in the same county (Rooks 54). When the state legislature determined that educational funding was to be decided by white local officials, Black teachers' salaries were immediately slashed and remained that way for years. By 1938, in that same county, Black teachers earned just over $8000 (for teaching 8483 students) while white teachers earned nearly $60,000 (for teaching fewer than 2000 students) (54).

Black schools had to overcome significant obstacles to educate Black children. Black students not only received inadequate state and local funding to fuel their education as demonstrated in per-student funding disparities, but they had access to fewer schools compared with white children. Because they were actively denied an education, Black children had to go to great lengths to get an education beyond the eighth grade and indeed their difficulty in doing so was by design. Political science professor Peter Irons notes:

A report on secondary education for Blacks in 1933 showed that between them, the states of Florida, Louisiana, Mississippi, and South Carolina had a total of 16 Black high schools accredited for four-year study. This report also noted that "89 percent of all Negro secondary schools are essentially elementary schools with one or more years of secondary work included at the top—often at the expense of the lower school." Even the four-year high schools had few resources; they averaged just five full-time and two part-time teachers, and most often one of the teachers doubled as principal. Hardly any of these Black high schools offered science courses or had laboratories, and very few had courses in foreign languages, music, or art. Their curriculum was limited and their teachers had little training in academic subjects. (36)

As a result, very few of the Black children who finished grade school in the 1930s were able to attend high school because of the scarcity of Black-serving high schools and the scarcity of resources within them. In Mississippi and Georgia, a dismal 5 and 8 percent of Black children were enrolled in high school. Only in North Carolina did as many as 20 percent of Black children attend high school. In the 1950s, only one of every eight Black adults had completed high school, while four of ten whites had earned their diploma (Irons). This damning evidence of Black children being barred from further education provides context for understanding the necessity and difficulty of cultivating freedom choices among Black mothers. Moreover, it makes plain the distinction we make between freedom choices, which do not assume freedom or the freedom to choose, and the freedom of choice, which implies freedom and the freedom to choose. It illuminates the choices available to Black people and the limits of their agency in the face of systemic racism. Finally, it lays bare the constraints Black mothers faced as they pushed to enlarge the boundaries of their children's choices by ensuring they could access an education.

Despite the racial disparities in their educational outcomes, Black people pursued education with a vengeance. In 1870, 20 percent of American adults were illiterate, but 80 percent of Black adults were. In 1900, 44 percent of Black people remained illiterate. By 1969, 3.6 percent of Black people were illiterate compared to 0.7 percent of white people (National Center for Education Statistics). The difference in Black and white school enrollment rates narrowed from twenty-three points in

1900 to seven points in 1940. Enrollment rates continued to rise in the post-war period, and by the early 1970s, enrollment rates for white and Black people had risen to about 90 percent and have remained relatively stable since then (National Center for Education Statistics). Although these statistics hide disparities in the length of school enrollment Black children were permitted, the quality of education they were afforded, and their access to secondary education, they corroborate that education was seen as a vehicle to achieve a freedom not experienced by Black people living as second-class citizens in a country that established itself as a dominant economic power on the world stage by exploiting their labour and innumerable contributions under the chattel slavery system. Ample evidence exists not only about white hostility to Black education from slavery through Jim Crow, but also about African Americans' demand for education through teaching themselves (Williams), through public schooling (Moss), and by creating and transforming higher education institutions (Williamson-Lott). The testimonies shared below, of attending school despite being confined to apartheid education, also demonstrate the value African Americans placed on education. What is unique about these narratives is that they provide insight into apartheid education across generations; as mothers tell their own stories, they provide insight into their parents' decision-making about sending (or not sending) them to school. At the same time, they construe their perceptions of apartheid education from the position of mothers with their children. Their narratives are a powerful testament to how Black families ensured their children took advantage of the available educational opportunities while strategizing to improve their educational experiences.

We identify four structural barriers that produced apartheid education and obstructed Black mothers from ensuring their children had an education on par with their white counterparts: unequal school terms, inadequate educational resources, lack of access to transportation, and unequal numbers of schools.

Black Children Were Denied Access to Equal School Terms

Black children faced shortened school terms (as little as three months) compared with white children who received an average of nine months of education annually (Rooks). Several structural factors created racial disparities in school terms. For starters, white landowners controlled when school districts opened and closed Black schools. In general, white landowners did not believe Black children needed classroom instruction, rationalizing that Black children were needed in the fields. As a result, Black education revolved around the overrepresentation of Black people in agriculture, especially sharecropping. Almost all Black children in the South missed school to do farm work (Irons). Thelma Woods Nash was born and raised in Brown's Corner, Arkansas. As an adolescent, she worked with her father on the railroad and picked cotton on nearby farms. Thelma elucidated the political economy that gave birth to apartheid education by explaining the relationship between Black children's education and sharecropping: "Yeah, the white people would go on to school. They started on time now, but the Blacks, that's the way they were scheduled, convenient for the big farmers, see. Because those big farmers had like 300 and 400 and 500 acres of land, and all these people that lived on it if they said for the school not to start it wasn't going to start if you weren't through." Thelma continued, "And they had like two months of summer school in the summer. Maybe you would get, maybe three in the fall."

Second, landowners engaged in direct confrontation with teachers to prohibit Black children's school participation. Elizabeth Pointer remarked, "If you got a child and the man want him to work, he go and tell the teacher that 'this boy can't come to school right now cause he workin' for me,' and he'd go there and get him out of school and [laughs] make him go to the field ... how horrible it is when you have to, everything you do the man's got to approve it." Elizabeth described her own shorter school term compared to whites: "And we only went to school, we could not go to school until October. It would have to be after Columbus Day. And you know why? Because Mr. Childer's cotton had to be picked and gathered before the Black children went to school. And we started the school in October, the middle of October." Cora Randle Flemming (b. 1933) was born in Stallo, Mississippi, in the rural community on Chapel Hill. She articulated, "We'd go to school maybe eight, six months. We'd get out of school and go to the field and gather the crops. Then we'd go back to school when the crops and things were gathered, like a split session."

Elizabeth Tunage (b. 1932), born and raised in Fargo, Arkansas, talked about not understanding why Black children received shorter-terms.

> We went to school around six months in the winter. Now that was the only thing that was kind of aggravating and I couldn't understand. The white kids would start to school in September

and go 'til May. We didn't start school until sometime about the last of October or about the middle of November somewhere along in there, and we went until it was time to start in the fields in the spring.... I neber [sic] did understand why I couldn't go to school.

Delores Twillie Woods, born and raised in Colwell, Arkansas, added that Black children may not even get the shorter term they received if they were needed in the fields: "Like two months in the summer, and maybe three in the fall. It depended on how the cotton was developing. Like July and August. July and August, you went to school. And you know what? You may didn't get two months in the fall, because sometimes that cotton would.... You wouldn't be through chopping."

Some oral history interviewees connected Black children's inability to spend more time in school to their lesser educational attainment compared with white children. Arnette Davis remarked, "That's why there's such a lot of kids from the south have a problem with school, because they've never gone to school a full term." Similarly, Virginia Jackson Sutton (b. 1917), raised in Four Corners, Louisiana, associated her inability to stay in school to her and her sibling's inability to "learn too much." She remarked, "We went to school but I didn't learn too much because when I was in the third grade I stopped and went in the field, went to work in the field.... I think my oldest sister stopped school in the sixth or seventh. And my sister Emily, I don't know what grade she stopped in but she didn't learn much, her at all. No, she didn't learn too much at all."

Black Children Were Denied Equal Educational Resources

Not only did Black children not get the same amount of time in school as white children, but when they were in school, their schools and educational materials were subpar. Elizabeth Pointer talked about attending school in Alabama in the 1930s and 1940s and provides insight into the difficulties Black students and teachers faced:

Well, you know we were the janitors, the maid. We had the first two weeks of school we had to clean the school, clean around the school, and get the school in shape. So, we really didn't start our classes up until November.... I went to Chehaw elementary, it was a two-room school. It went through one through six grades. And one, two, three was in the same room. Four through six was in the same room. And two teachers. One teacher taught one through three, the other taught four through six…. We didn't have nothing at our school. They give the teachers some chalk and a couple of erasers for the board but no kind of supplies did we have. Not even heat. If your father didn't bring two loads of wood to that school then they make you go to the woods and gather wood and you, you not going to sit by the other children's fire.

Many Black children were educated in one-room schoolhouses. Cora Randle Flemming imparted, "The rural schools, the one-room schoolhouses. They had one or two teachers, maybe two teachers in the classroom. Maybe they had 150 kids and maybe two teachers." Black children not only learned in inferior environments and had a higher student-teacher ratio but often lacked textbooks or relied on hand-me-down books from white schools. Ira Lee Jones shared: "We used the same books but they were always what we called the hand me downs. They were raggedy books…. Our teachers always had problems filling in the parts of the lesson that was missing from the book." One woman shared how at the beginning of the school term, they would have to erase the racial epithets written into some of the textbooks by white students who knew that Black students would be given their old books. Their teacher armed them with tape for when they ripped the pages.

Delores Twillie Woods noted that Black children had to use the facilities at white schools to engage in extracurricular activities: "The Black schools did not have, we did not have a gym or nothing or no place for a football field for the boys to play football…. And they used to do that and then finally they built a football field over for the Black people to have." Delores shared that she was taught little Black history.

> Oh no, nothing. We didn't study Black History until we got in high school. It wasn't too much then. We had one class. And then our teachers didn't know to say, well, it's important that everybody take Black History. They get a mandatory subject like some of them, like American History and things like that. And that was what you called an elective and you could take it if you wanted to and I wanted to take it. So, I took Black History, but a lot of people didn't. Had one class of Black History. That's right. Not many of us got a chance to really read about Black History.

In contrast, other women reported being taught Black history by their teachers. Daisy Livingston (b. 1926) who was born and raised in Greenwood, Mississippi, shared, "We were taught about everything, but our teachers taught us mostly about black history with their own books or their own knowledge and with the Bible." Daisy talked about the impact of one teacher in particular:

> Then we had a teacher, Mrs. Brooks, who taught us that—she said, "What goes around come around." She told us that the Egyptians and whatnot were our brothers and there were a time when they had like we were in slavery and made like second-class citizens, that we had done that to a Caucasian race at one time in history. And, I don't know, that we came from queens and kings. A lot of us—I wasn't the only one. There were more of us. Yes, we felt like we was as good as anybody. We sure did.

Women often remarked about how Black teachers created opportunities from limited resources in terms of educating Black students with a fraction of the resources white students and teachers received. Lola Hayes Hendrick (b. 1932), who was born and raised in Birmingham, Alabama, exemplified this perspective. Lola spoke eloquently about how Black teachers were committed to the success of Black students despite having few resources to work with:

> Elementary school, we went to a little wooden building. Everything was segregated then.... We had very little to work with, very bad books and things that would be torn that were provided for us to read. We had excellent teachers. We have to really give praises to the Black teachers that we had during that era. They were committed to our being better students, or equal students on the part of the same level with the whites, with less accommodation for us. They taught us more than what was in them books. They taught us how to prepare ourselves, to the best that we could be with whatever talent that we had. We did not have access to a lot of cultural things during my high school era. Elementary school was just basic reading, writing, and arithmetic, and when we got to high school, we had very little cultural things, other than the choirs. At Parker [a high school], we did have a drama club and we did have a speech club, but as far as going in the community to do things, we did not have as much exposure as the white student.

Bernice Magruder White also noted that Black teachers taught them well given their shorter time frame to cover material: "I completed eight grades in the rural area. Now, one thing I can say, our school time was much shorter, six months probably the most, but during this time we didn't have a lot of subjects, but we did cover those real well."

Black Children Had Access to Fewer Schools

Black children didn't have access to the same number of schools as white children, especially high schools. While schools for kindergarten through eighth grade were more readily available, Black communities (1) often lacked a high school, (2) relied on one high school to educate all of its students, or (3) were forced to bus children to a Black high school outside of their community.

Sue Kelker Russell (b. 1909) was born in Milton, Florida, and grew up there. She explained how some Black communities had no high school at all:

> We couldn't go to school with the whites. We had to go to Escambia County, to Pensacola to school. We didn't have a high school in Milton and we had to leave Milton for Escambia or go somewhere else if we wanted to finish high school. And, that was about, you knowed you had the race problem, but it was just about, I guess, like every other, small southern town. Whites had their areas and Blacks theirs. Blacks was, of course, subservient to whites, so to speak.

Similarly, Ira Lee Jones commented: "They had an elementary school over [in Birmingham] but did not have a ... high school at that time."

Ferdie Walker explained that regardless of what part of town Black children lived in, they all had to attend the one Black high school:

> Fort Worth was separated for Black people into lots of different areas because many Black people lived on each side of town, but I lived on the east side which was really a relatively poor neighborhood.... There was one Black high school. So, all of the Black kids from all over town went to one Black high school. And there were elementary schools in each section of town for Black children. I never had a white teacher in my life, until I got in college.

Cora Randle Flemming remarked about the dearth of schools available in Mississippi at the higher levels: "We had from pre-primer through eighth grade. To us at that time, it was good, because we didn't know anything different from that. But then when we went to high school, I found a lot of things were different from the rural community schools."

Bernice White expressed feeling "lucky" to attend high school:

> But I do think I was somewhat lucky. If I go back just a little bit, before we left the rural area, I was sent to, when I got fifteen, then I had finished—well, fourteen, I'm sorry. I finished elementary school. There was no school that I could go beyond eighth grade, and so if you go to school, you had to live with someone or they had boarding schools. So I was sent to a boarding school in Coahoma County. The name of that school was Coahoma Agricultural High School, and I finished ninth and tenth grades there. Then I came to Indianola to go to school, because my people were well established.

Black Children Were Denied Access to Transportation

It was commonplace for Black children living in the rural south to walk miles each day to get to school, while white children often rode on taxpayer-supported buses. Rooks notes, "Black parents were repeatedly told by educators that if they wanted their children to ride on school buses then they should be free to purchase them, fill them with gasoline, hire a driver, and repair them—all at their own expense. However, there would be no tax dollars spent on the transportation of Black children" (84).

Daisy Livingston commented: "There were a school out there with one teacher, but I didn't attend that school. I walked about five or six miles, maybe farther, to school. I walked first to McLaurin Street School for elementary, and then you passed by Nicholson Elementary." Similarly, Elizabeth Tunage spoke about Black children's lack of access to transportation to and from school: "And another thing, we walked to school and I thought that was maybe because we didn't have far to go, the reason why we were walking, because it was something like a mile, mile and a half for most of us that went to school." Elizabeth Pointer shared that she too walked to school: "Every day and back no matter if it was storming. We could not ride the buses although we were paying taxes.

But we couldn't ride those buses nothing rode the bus but the whites."

Lola Hayes Hendrick shared that the Black children in her community were only provided transportation when they attended high school, of which there were only two that they could attend:

> Yeah, we had to walk. There was no public transportation, no specials [buses] to take us. We had to walk to school. The only time we had specials was when we got to high school. They would bus us to high school, and that was only because they had us segregated to Parker or Ullman. Those were the only two high schools in the city of Birmingham that you could graduate from. Ullman was a two-year high school; Parker was a four-year. So those people who lived on the north side went to Parker the whole four years, but we lived over on the south side, so we had to go to Ullman two years and the other two years at Parker.

Instead of walking, Ira Lee Jones took the city bus to school, which she had to pay for:

> The only segregation that I can recount of my early age was going to school 'cause we had to pass all the white high school to get to where the negroes went to school and from where I lived....We had to ride the bus ... not a school bus but the city owned bus and if it was snowing or raining whatever we had problems getting to and from the bus and the white kids didn't seem to have that problem.

Elizabeth Pitts pointed out that both Black children and Black teachers walked to school: "We had to walk to school. We didn't have transportation. We didn't have buses. And the teacher she had to walk too."

Strategies of Resistance: Cultivating Freedom Choices

> Well, I tell you I just wish that we all had the same chance. I mean, we just don't have the chances that the white people have. They get the better breaks. We just don't get the good breaks. I mean, you may see one out of ten, they get a good break. But we don't have even the opportunities now. The kids in school, they don't have the opportunity that the whites have. They don't have that offer. And they don't know about it..... And I believe it'll always be there."
>
> —Elcie Snorton Eaves

Elcie Snorton Eaves (b. 1928) observed how systemic racism differentially ordered the opportunities available in American society by race. She made the above remarks in 1995, and twenty-six years later, what she believed had come to pass—African Americans still experience racial disparities in educational outcomes and opportunities ("we don't have the chances [or good breaks] that the white people have"). The US prides itself on its freedoms. But its freedoms are not only limited to certain domains, constrained by laws and social expectations, and defined by external boundaries, but are also limited to certain people. Black people's choices during the Jim Crow era were intensely constrained at best and nonexistent at worst. As the stories above indicate, Black mothers gave their children freedom choices by ensuring they attended school at all, which was significant given the economic pressures faced by Black families, the social control whites exerted over Black educations, shorter school terms, lack of transportation, inadequate resources, and fewer schools. The stories above do not reveal how Black mothers facilitated their children's educational pursuits. We show that Black mothers leveraged their sweat equity (meaning they tapped into their own labour rather than relied on their children's), tapped into their mutual aid networks, challenged landowners, and insisted on prioritizing their children's education even when their partners did not—all to give their children the one thing they knew could provide the freedom to have choices beyond those they would likely have without it: an education.

Jessie Lee Chassion (b. 1926) illustrated the use of different strategies across generations to increase children's educational attainment. As a child, Jessie was sent to live near relatives to get an education: "I wasn't living there. I was living here. I could walk to school. See you couldn't send your children to, they had a little school out there, a little country school but if it rained too much the children couldn't go to school because there was too much water. So, I came to school here and I lived here. I had family here so I could go to school." When she had her own son, she stressed the importance of education over work for her son, despite needing the extra income produced by his labour:

> Because I have a son that did restaurant and my son I let him work with me after school washing dishes because he needed the little extra money. And one day he, he didn't like to go to school to start off with and one day he told me that the man said if he wasn't going to school he would give him a full-time job and believe it or not I made him quit. I didn't quit and I needed for him to work but he didn't want to go and this wasn't going to help me none and I wanted him to finish school so I said, "Well, as of today you don't come back."

Jessie showed how mothers worked hard so that their children could have a better life by focussing on obtaining an education. Similarly, Alice Dunnigan (b. 1906) who lived in Russellville, Kentucky, spoke repeatedly of her lifelong devotion to education: "One of the things I remember best is … my interest in education. I always wanted to go to school, even when I was only three or four years old. When my big brother would go to school, leaving me at home, I would always cry." Her earnestness impressed her brother's teachers, who let her start school at age four, when she began official schooling at age six, she was a grade ahead of her peers. Despite the long distance to school, Alice made the trek daily. If it rained or snowed, Alice recalled her mother forbidding her from walking, and Alice would stay home and "[cry] all day." Alice knew firsthand how education could be a way to improve one's life. She went on to become a teacher, mother, activist, economist, and journalist. She laboured to help her son finish college: "I discovered that I couldn't depend upon my husband for support. Our son, Robert William (Bob), was in his second year of college when my mother died. I worked hard, and kept him in school until he finished at Kentucky State College."

Oral history interviewees reported being encouraged by mothers more than fathers to pursue and complete their education. Bernice Magruder White reflected on how her mother emphasized education: "My mother … she was the one that pushed education. What my father was trying to do was just find food and things that we need in the home." Bernice's mother pushed education despite her poor health and did so more than her father:

> Well, let me tell you, she passed in '54 at the age of forty-seven. She was not real active in working because she was somewhat ill, and we didn't know what was wrong with her. A strange thing, you don't know. We thought our mother was lazy because she didn't like to cook. But my grandfather did like to cook, and so that's why we kind of hung around at his home. But my mother had an enlarged heart. I think she grew up with that, and that was a problem. But it was years, we were grown when we found that out. She assured that we went to school. She was the one that looked to find out what school we could afford to go to, and whereas my daddy, I don't know whether it would have mattered with him if we had continued on or not, but it did matter with her. She was, as I said, somewhat in the background a lot and just believed in going to school.

Ira Lee Jones talked about the length her mother, who worked as a laundress, went to make sure that she and her brother received an education:

> Getting to and from school was not the greatest thing. It was a mile away from our house and mother didn't want us to walk so most of the time she would put a quarter's worth of gas in the car and take us. You know a quarter's worth of gas at that time was a lot of gas. And she would take us back and forwards to school and it was fun to see her learn to drive. And she also bought us a piano taking other children back and forwards to school, they'd pay her a quarter and she would take them and she paid for a piano like that. So, we could take music.

History professor Jacqueline Jones featured the story of the educator William Pickens, who speaking from experience, declared, "Many an educated Negro owes his enlightenment to the toil and sweat of a mother." A common practice used by Black mothers to support their children's education is evident in the saying "chickens for shoes." Mothers used the money they earned selling eggs and chickens to buy shoes for their children so that they could attend school in the winter (Jones 91).

Likewise, educator Rossa B. Cooley moved to St. Helena Island in 1901 to set up a school. She found that some Black mothers were concerned about ensuring that their daughters did not experience the same fate they had endured. Jones shared Cooley's observation: "For example, born and raised in slavery, the Sea Island woman Chloe had "one idea" for her daughter Clarissa and that was "an education that meant going to school and away from all the drudgery, the chance to wear pretty clothes any day in the week, and as her utmost goal, the Latin and algebra offered by the early Negro schools in their zeal to prove the capacity of liberated Blacks" (91).

Similar to other research, we found that Black mothers were more likely to emphasize education for girls than boys. Jones observed that while girls engaged in some type of field and domestic labour at an early age, parents excused them more often and for longer periods (compared to their brothers) to attend school. In 1910, the census indicated: "Negro girls and younger women have received at least such elementary school training as is represented by the ability to write, more generally than have Negro boys and men" (Jones 92). Between 1880 and 1915, school attendance rates among Black females remained higher than among males, producing an early form of the "farmer's daughter effect." In the fifteen-to-twenty-year age bracket, only seven Black males attended school for every ten females (Jones 87).

Elizabeth Pitts was born and raised in Greenwood, Mississippi. When asked if she left school to pick cotton, Elizabeth responded, "No, uh uh, I didn't have to but some of the guys, some of the bigger boys did. They had to leave school to go to work, but I was fortunate enough I didn't have to leave to go to work." The interviewer continued, "So did they treat the girls different than they treated the boys?" Elizabeth replied, "Well, the boys lived on plantations too so if there was something to do they had to stop and go do it, you know, like plow or haul, whatever the boss had for them to do, uh-huh, they had to leave and go do that. But we never did, the girls never did leave school."

Black mothers also had to make decisions about whether to expand their children's choices by integrating schools. Delores Twillie Woods signed her children up to integrate their school:

> So shortly after they started marching and doing all this stuff, they were able to help them to integrate schools…. And freedom of choice and it was that I could sign my child up to go over there

> to that school if I wanted to. And so, they did that like what, about a couple of years? So that freedom of choice must have started about 1966 or '67, 'cause I remember my daughter graduated from over there in 1968. My daughter graduated and I had a girl and a boy. This was before they had totally integrated the schools. And so, then they had freedom of choice and they thought the Black people would be afraid to sign their children up to go over there. So, I signed mine up. And so, they was telling me, well, they not too good a student. You going to sign them up. I said, "I can't sign one up without signing the other one up" ... But she did good over there.

While Woods spoke about her willingness to allow her children to be on the frontlines of school integration, even when white people thought Black parents would be too scared to do so, not all mothers were eager to integrate white schools. Elizabeth Pointer refused to let her children integrate a school. "I wouldn't never sent my children down there ... I may as well send my children to the rattlesnakes.... I was not going to have my daughter mistreated and people throwing things on her like they did a lot of little, 'cause I'd a went down there and they'd a had me killed or in jail. 'Cause they sure don't touch my daughter, they'd a been a dead bird."

Conclusion

Consistent with research on how Black mothers prepare their children for success and protect them from anti-Black racism (Diamond and Gomez; Elliott and Reid; Herelle), we demonstrated how Black mothers living in Jim Crow used formal and informal education to prepare their children and to keep them safe from harm. Extending this area of research, we demonstrate that while several intervening factors likely shape how Black mothers use formal education to facilitate their children's success, minimizing hindrances and restraints that shape children's educational choices and expanding their available options is central to their strategizing. We contend that the practice of cultivating freedom choices stresses that individuals both have options and agency and that they are constrained by their social context. Freedom choices acknowledge these constraints, as Black mothers push to enlarge the boundaries of their children's choices by ensuring they can access an education. Black mothers knew that their children would need an education to transcend Jim Crow racism. Black children attended schools that received less funding than the schools where white students were educated. As a result, the learning environments in Black schools were too often inadequate despite the efforts of Black communities, school boards, and teachers to give Black children the best education they could.

Black children often learned in dilapidated school buildings, lacked textbooks or relied on hand-me-down books from white schools, and studied in overcrowded schools with too many students per teacher. More Black schools than white ones had only one teacher to handle all grade levels. Black schools were also more likely to have all grades together in one room. Moreover, because of how agricultural work structured and exploited the lives of many Black workers and families, it was difficult for Black children to enroll and remain in school because of competing work demands and financial constraints. Still, Black mothers across generations facilitated their children's education by emphasizing education over work and stressing education even when their partners did not. They also sent their children to live with loved ones when they could receive a better education. Some Black mothers sought to integrate schools to access better education for their children, while others resisted their children being at the forefront of school integration because of concerns about their safety. Finally, Black mothers made sure that they educated their girl children, who were much more likely to become educators and stress education not only for their own children but for all Black children.

During the Jim Crow era, Black mothers understood, even if their children did not, that they had to be alive to take advantage of these opportunities. So, they used informal education to keep them safe. Like their contemporary counterparts, Black mothers raising children during Jim Crow understood that their children could be insulted, assaulted, or killed just because of the colour of their skin. Like their contemporary counterparts, Black mothers raising children during Jim Crow tried to protect and prepare their children wherever their Black bodies took them in the US. Across time and space, Black mothers understand that anti-Black racism manifests in their children's premature and violent deaths at the hands of police and white vigilantes and racists. Thus, Black mothers in our study taught their children restraint *and* resistance and set them forth in a world that they knew would most assuredly test whether they knew which strategy to employ when faced with instances of anti-Black racism. As they faced "For Whites Only" signs, the degradations of white children riding on school buses hurling racial slurs, trash, and rocks at them, and the whites who used their position at the top of the racial hierarchy to terrorize them in ways big and small, Black children frequently pulled from the arsenal of strategies that their mothers explicitly and implicitly taught them.

Endnotes

1. "Since the 1920s, white women's labor force participation has increased substantially due to the entrance of married white women into the workforce (Boustan and Collins 2013), but has only exceeded Black women's participation once, briefly, in 1994 (Bureau of Labor Statistics 2015a)."
2. Black women experienced relative wage gains of 16.2 in the 1940s and 15.8 percentage points in the 1960s. In the 1940s, Black women's weekly wages increased from $13 to $24, and Black to white female earnings increased from .44 to .59, meaning Black women earned 59 percent of what white women did (Bailey and Collins).
3. Earnings are lower than white women and men, and Black men.

Works Cited

Alson, Julianna G., et al., "Incorporating Measures of Structural Racism into Population Studies of Reproductive Health in the United States: A Narrative Review." *Health Equity*, vol. 5, 2021, pp. 49–58.

Althoff, Lukas, and Hugo Reichardt. "Jim Crow and Black Economic Progress After Slavery." *The Quarterly Journal of Economics*, vol. 139, 2024, pp. 2279–330.

Bailey, Amy, and Tolnay, Stewart. *Lynched: The Victims of Southern Mob Violence*. University of North Carolina Press, 2015.

Bailey, Martha, and William Collins. "The Wage Gains of African-American Women in the 1940s." *The Journal of Economic History*, vol. 66, no. 3, 2006, pp. 737–77.

Collins, Patricia Hill. *Black Feminist Thought: Knowledge, Consciousness, and the Politics of Empowerment*. Routledge, 2000.

Diamond, John B., and Kimberley Gomez. "African American Parents' Educational Orientations: The Importance of Social Class and Parents' Perceptions of Schools." *Education and Urban Society*, vol. 36, 2004, pp. 383–427.

Dominguez, Tyan Parker. "Adverse Birth Outcomes in African American Women: The Social Context of Persistent Reproductive Disadvantage." *Social Work in Public Health*, vol. 26, 2011, pp. 3–16.

Dunaway, Wilma A. *The African-American Family in Slavery and Emancipation*. Cambridge University Press, 2003.

Elliott, Sinikka, and Megan Reid. "Low-Income Black Mothers Parenting Adolescents in the Mass Incarceration Era: The Long Reach of Criminalization." *American Sociological Review*, vol. 84, 2019, pp. 197–219.

Gates, Henry Louis. *Stony the Road: Reconstruction, White Supremacy, and the Rise of Jim Crow*. Penguin Publishing Group, 2019.

Geronimus, Arline T., et al. "'Weathering' and Age Patterns of Allostatic Load Scores Among Blacks and Whites in the United States." *American Journal of Public Health*, vol. 96, 2006, pp. 826–33.

Goldin, Claudia. "Female Labor Force Participation: The Origin of Black and White Differences, 1870 and 1880." *The Journal of Economic History*, vol. 37, no. 1, 1977, pp. 87–108.

Herelle, Tarsha I. "To Protect and to Prepare: Black Mothers' School-Selection Decision-Making. Race, Ethnicity and Education." *Race Ethnicity and Education*, vol. 28, no. 1, 2022, pp. 76–94.

Irons, Peter H. *Jim Crow's Children: The Broken Promise of the Brown Decision*. Penguin, 2004.

Jones, Jacqueline. *Labor of Love, Labor of Sorrow: Black Women, Work and the Family, from Slavery to the Present*. Basic Books, 2009.

Maloney, Thomas. "African Americans in the Twentieth Century." EH.Net Encyclopedia, 14 Jan. 2002, https://eh.net/encyclopedia/african-americans-in-the-twentieth-century/. Accessed 23 Dec. 2024.

Moss, Hilary J. *Schooling Citizens: The Struggle for African American Education in Antebellum America*. University of Chicago Press, 2009.

National Center for Education Statistics. "Literacy from 1870 to 1979." *NCES*, https://nces.ed.gov/naal/lit_history.asp. Accessed 23 Dec. 2024.

Paul, Mark, et al. *Returns in the Labor Market: A Nuanced View of Penalties at the Intersection of Race and Gender.* Washington Center for Equitable Growth, 2018.

Pittman, LaShawnDa. *Grandmothering While Black: A Twenty-First-Century Story of Love, Coercion, and Survival.* University of California Press, 2023.

Rooks, Noliwe. *Cutting School: Privatization, Segregation, and the End of Public Education.* The New Press, 2017.

Ross, Loretta, et al., eds. *Radical Reproductive Justice: Foundation, Theory, Practice, Critique.* Feminist Press at CUNY, 2017.

Roux, Mathilde. "5 Facts About Black Women in the Labor Force." U.S. Department of Labor Blog. Washington: Women's Bureau, 2021.

Ruggles, Steve. "The Origins of African-American Family Structure." *American Sociological Review*, vol. 59, no. 1, 1994, pp. 136–51.

Simmons, LaKisha Michelle. *Crescent City Girls: The Lives of Young Black Women in Segregated New Orleans.* The University of North Carolina, 2015.

Singh, Gopal K., and Stella M. Yu. "Infant Mortality in the United States, 1915-2017: Large Social Inequalities Have Persisted for Over a Century." *International journal of MCH and AIDS*, vol. 8, no. 1, 2019, pp. 19–31.

Sister Song. https://www.sistersong.net/mission. Accessed 23 Dec. 2024.

Southern Poverty Leadership Council. "Mississippi's Broken Promise—A Timeline." SPLC, 23 May 2017, https://www.splcenter.org/20170523/mississippi%E2%80%99s-broken-education-promise-%E2%80%93-timeline. Accessed 23 Dec. 2024.

Strauss, Anselm, and Juliet Corbin. *Basics of Qualitative Research: Grounded Theory Procedures and Techniques.* Sage Publications, Inc, 1990.

Wilkerson, Isabel. *Caste: The Origins of Our Discontents.* Random House Publishing Group, 2020.

Williams, Heather A. *Self-Taught: African American Education in Slavery and Freedom.* University of North Carolina Press, 2005.

Williamson-Lott, Joy Ann. *Jim Crow Campus: Higher Education and the Struggle for a New Southern Social Order.* Teachers College Press, 2018.

3.

A Lesson I Did Not Teach

Jameka Hartley

I did not teach her
that the police
are the "good guys"

I did not teach her
who the police were
before she was taught to love Chase on Paw Patrol

I did not teach her to play jail
nor to call the police for help

I did not teach her that the "good guys"
catch
the "bad guys"

Yet this is her present reality

Her affinity for them is unsettling to me
Because I know it is not reciprocal

The police do not hold a fondness
in their hearts for little Blackgirls
The oath to protect and to serve
has a melanated loophole

I have yet to teach her
that being Black
too often makes us
the "bad guys"

Her understanding of cops and robbers
Be life or death

I will teach her that everything
doesn't warrant the police
but instead
collective care and community

Together, I hope, one day
we only talk
about who the police
used to be

4.

Known Black

Jameka Hartley

I don't remember when I learned I was Black
I been Black
Be Black
Forever will be Black

My mama only bought me Black dolls
And books with Black characters
The only Santas in our house were Black
The Christmas angels, too!

She only bought greeting cards with Black people on them
And if for some reason she couldn't find a card with a Black face
She'd use a colored pencil and would color it brown.

Black people were the center of my mama's world
And she made sure they were the center of mine
Now it's my turn to mama
and I do the same

We read Black stories about Black girls
like Mae (Jemison) and Katherine (Johnson)
We recite the Nguzo Saba

We buy Black
Teach Black
Be Black
Been Black
Forever will be Black

5.

Nana Would Pull Magic from Out Her Pocketbook

Devynity

Nana would pull magic from outta her pocketbook

Candy

Chocolates

Rainbonnets

Here, put this on

When the sky opened up

And an umbrella too

Lipstick and mirror

Lotion

And napkins to clean up whatever mess there was

Because there will always be mess

Some nose to blow, some seat to wipe so one can sit

Some set of lips to dab at in the corners

Magic, I tell you, from outta that pocketbook

A comb

And a pen for writing with

Some kinda piece of paper for just in case one might need to jot something down

And something for the breath cuz she knows that a first impression is everything and it's

behooved her to have at least a piece of gum on hand in the event of such an occasion

For it must be a pleasure to meet her acquaintance

A magician with no hat

No wand and no rabbit

Just magic

Magic in that bag, I tell you

With straps on her shoulders

Sinful to place it on the floor

For so revered that well-stocked appendage

Indeed upended all others

And we learned to be prepared

From that magic that she'd pull from up outta that pocketbook

6.

Mama Illusion

Toya Leigh Groves

    What's in that bag?

lip gloss smeared with liner of the eyes
      to draw on dams
         Cuz damn
you forgot to get milk and oh the guilt
                to sit with the forgot that remembers
            the reality that really you aint got it
          couldn't get it   never had it cuz
              the EBT card
        that charges in the leather coils of
        your fake coach bag jumped out in
                the rain

    as you ran for the bus
    clutched in your hand
carrying crumpled-up welfare packets
      Time to renew
    Not renew as in rebirth
  but renew interrogation of the soul
    questions of trickery
    sliding down and out
of eyes and over noses and nods
    that never see just report
      on the lines

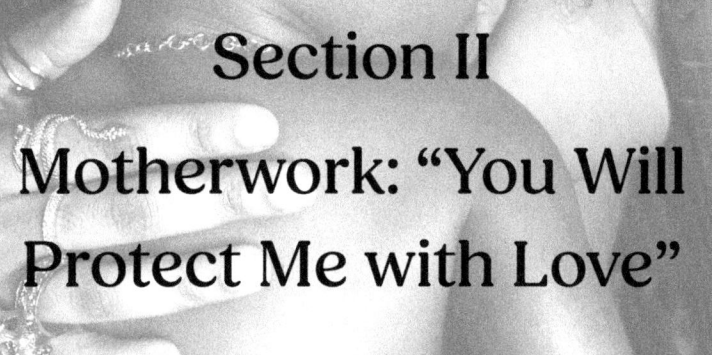

Section II

Motherwork: "You Will Protect Me with Love"

7.

Dear Mama

Alexis Henderson

I know these times are hard
And keeping strong cannot be compared.
The world seems not to be smiling,
But you Mama, I know will be there.
You will hug me and keep me safe,
You will protect me with love.
They always say stay strong Mama,
But this is what I'm thinking of...
Take a break, relax your mind.
Let go of the things that are not kind.
Don't stress Mama, meditate and pray.
When things get rough, reach out.
Because I am here with you every day.
I am you and you of me.
Your mind is the creator of what you believe.
So believe greatly, have faith, do try.
Because I love you, Mama.
My love for you will never die.

8.

Hard Questions

Traci-Ann Wint

The morning after she turns five, she asks me who will watch the man's daughter when her Mummy is in a meeting. A part of me wants to pretend I don't know which man she's talking about because that would be easier than answering the hard questions, but pretense is pointless. George Floyd's face has been plastered all over our television screen for days. We've been watching footage of people filling the streets of cities all over the United States, holding each other with one hand and signs that say "Black Lives Matter" with the other.

She's just learning to read. She wants to know what the signs say.

We sound out syllables, and I try to explain.

This is a prekindergarten reading lesson of the strangest kind.

The measured voices of newscasters rehashing the minutes leading up to George Floyd's death overwhelm our tiny living room. The twenty-four-hour news cycle is filled with new-to-her words like "loot" and "injustice" and "tear gas" and "riot." On screen there is fire, smoke, and broken glass, officers of the peace dressed in funereal black, holding shields, and wielding batons. Everything is curious. The questions keep coming, and I keep stumbling through inadequate explanations of why a white police officer kneeled on a Black man's neck for eight minutes and forty-six seconds until he stopped breathing.

"I wish the police knew that the men aren't mean," she says.

I decide not to tell her that things like this happen to women, too.

I don't know if it is the right decision. I don't say anything about the assumed meanness.

Days earlier, when we made signs to take to the march in our city, I asked my daughter what she wanted her sign to say.

"People should not be killed. Not even Black people," she said with the gleeful assurance only children possess.

I typed "Black Lives Matter" in Times New Roman bold, printed it on a white letter-sized sheet, stuck it onto orange construction paper, and gave her that instead.

"Not even Black people" felt like too much to digest, too much to explain.

Not. Even. Black. People.

The morning after she turns five, a full week's worth of sleeps after the march, she throws the question at me over cold coffee and soggy cereal.

"Who will watch the man's daughter?"

I swallow and shuffle and sip and tell her that the girl will be taken care of by her uncles, or aunties, or grandma, or maybe even a babysitter. I assure her that there are friends and relatives, a whole community of care.

It is not enough.

Now she follows her father around the house as though if out of her sight, he might go poof and disappear.

"When will Daddy be back?" she asks in three-minute intervals whenever he's left the house.

"What do you need? Can Mummy help?" I reply feeling guilty about the exasperation in my voice.

"No," she says. Firm. "I want a Daddy hug. I need to smell his beard."

Children are weird.

"That man Mummy" she still repeats—"Who will watch his daughter?"

9.

Ay-Yai! Black Mother Leadership and Storytelling Traditions

Stephanie Fearon

Introduction

Black mothers worldwide embody a rich tradition of using stories to mobilize and organize for Black liberation (Dei et al. 13; Maynard 163). Our maternal stories challenge us, and others, to bear witness to our collective resistance against the oppressions levied against our children, families, and communities. We use our stories to help plot, map, remember, and interpret the archives of the everyday Black experience. In *Talkin and Testifyin: The Language of Black America*, Geneva Smitherman articulates storytelling as a rhetorical strategy used by Black communities to convey broad, theoretical observations about Black life through concrete stories (Smitherman 150; Toliver 507). We use our maternal stories, comprising personal and cultural stories, and metanarratives to ask and answer epistemological and ontological questions in our voices (Fearon 26). Our longstanding tradition of storytelling affirms our shared humanity and further connects Black people, especially Black mothers, across the diaspora.

Given the importance of excavating and amplifying stories told by Black mothers, this article focuses on how Black Canadian mothers use storytelling traditions to negotiate and reconfigure their roles as leaders at their children's schools. This chapter presents insights obtained from ten in-depth interviews with Black Canadian mothers. These interviews, reconfigured into the creative nonfiction story *Ay-Yai*, capture how participants used storytelling to reimagine their motherwork as a form of educational leadership. The following questions guide this chapter:

- How do Black Canadian mothers use Black storytelling traditions to conceptualize their motherwork?

- How do Black Canadian mothers draw on the art of storytelling to shape their understanding and practice of leadership at their children's schools?

This chapter begins with an overview of Black Canadian mothers' historical and present-day activism work in Canadian schools. In so doing, the chapter contextualizes Black Canadian mothers within the country's racial, gendered, and class hierarchies as well as movements for Black lives. Drawing on the research-driven creative nonfiction story *Ay-Yai*, this chapter critically explores Black Canadian mothers' use of storytelling traditions to impart and practice educational leadership skills. The chapter concludes with a call to action for scholars and educational practitioners to uphold Black Canadian mothers as trusted educational leaders within their homes, communities, and children's schools.

Researcher's Positionality

I am a Black Canadian mother, educator, and researcher of Black Jamaican descent. As a Black woman and mother, I occupy dual positions within the study explored in this chapter—an insider and an outsider. I leveraged my lived experiences as a Black Canadian mother to establish trusting relationships with the Black mothers who participated in the study. I understand Black Canadians' distrust in engaging in research tied to institutions. Black communities, dating back to their early interactions with public Canadian institutions, have been marred with violence and harm throughout research processes (REDE4 Black Lives). Black community organizations and research groups, including Research Evaluation Data Ethics Protocol for Black Populations, stress the importance of conducting ethical, beneficial, and relevant research on the health and wellbeing of people of African descent in Canada (REDE4 Black Lives). As such, my research and mothering practices are committed to exploring how scholarship on Black women's motherwork can further support Black mother leaders working in our children's schools and communities.

Black Canadian Mothers and the Canadian Education System: A Historical and Contemporary Review

Black Canadian mothers have long been at the forefront of liberation movements. For centuries, we have leveraged our motherwork to assert our children's physical safety and wellbeing in Canadian schools. Our maternal stories chronicle our deep-rooted activism within our diverse Black Canadian communities, some of which stretches back to the beginning of settler colonialism and enslavement in the country (James et al. 33). In Canada, our stories trace the early activism of Black mothers who in response to the rejection of their children from public schools in the nineteenth century created their own academic institutions with little assistance from white school officials. Our narratives uphold Black Canadian mother and teacher Mary Ann Shadd Cary and community mother and educator Mary Bibb as leaders who spearheaded these separate schools for Black children (Aladejebi 8).

We continue this legacy of using our maternal stories to archive our present-day activism in Canadian schools. In 2019, Shada Mohamed led a group of Black mothers demanding the Alberta Ministry of Education to take action against anti-Black racism plaguing their children's schools (McGarvey). Mohamed and fellow mothers accused school officials of denying the existence of anti-Black racism in public schools and ignoring its negative impact on Black children's health and achievement. When sharing her story with the community, Mohamed declared, "I've been into the school every time there's been an issue, I address it right after school and address it with the principal. Nobody seems to take this seriously. It's a joke" (qtd. In McGarvey). Also in 2019, Edmonton school officials called an eleven-year-old Black boy a gang member because he wore a durag (Konguavi). When the boy's mother, Una Momulu, sought redress from the principal, school officials called the police on her and later prohibited her from entering her son's school. In addition to her son being racially profiled, Momulu recounted to the community that she was "painted as an angry Black woman" and threatened with legal action by the school board (qtd. In Konguavi). At a board meeting, Momulu said, "It is time to acknowledge that this entire incident has to do with race from the very beginning" (qtd. In Konguavi).

Black Lives Matter movements across North America continue the tradition of using maternal stories to organize for Black life. For example, Black Lives Matter movements in Canada have amplified impassioned maternal stories shared by Black Canadian mothers like Leisa Lewis. Lewis, mother of nineteen-year-old Dafonte Miller, spoke out about her son's recovery from a brutal beating by an off-duty police officer resulting in her son being traumatized and blinded (Reddekopp). Lewis told the public, "Two, three more blows, my son could have been dead" (qtd. in Reddekopp). Another Black Canadian mother, who chose to remain anonymous to protect her daughter's identity, used maternal storytelling to detail the dehumanization of her six-year-old daughter by police and education officials following her child's handcuffing at school (Cheung and Sienkiewicz). Black Lives Matter took up these maternal stories to galvanize the public to take action and uphold the sanctity of Black life.

By positioning our stories of liberation work within the historical context, we better understand Black Canadian mothers' experiences in the public education system as being shaped by a continuum of anti-Black racism. We also further appreciate Black Canadian mothers' enduring commitment to organizing with other Black mothers to uphold their children's dignity within the education system and that of the entire community. Much like Mary Ann Shadd Cary, Mary Bibb, and other early Black Canadian mother leaders who have come before us, we continue to head resistance movements against the harm inflicted on our children and families within the public education system and beyond. Black Lives Matter movements continue to draw on maternal stories to rally communities and society-at-large for Black liberation.

Arts-Informed Narrative Methodology

I used an arts-informed narrative methodology to explore Black Canadian mothers' use of storytelling to assert their roles as leaders within their children's school. Arts-informed narrative research relies on empirical data informed by the literary genre and comprises personal narration and cultural stories (Onuora 3). I join other researchers-turned-creative writers, like Adwoa Ntozake Onuora, to practise meaning-making by storying memories relayed from conversations with participants (Onuora). For this study, I engaged in what Toni Morrison calls "literary archaeology" (Morrison 112). I used information, descriptions, and direct quotations from participants' transcripts and reconstructed them into a series of creative nonfiction stories that take readers on a narrative journey through lived experiences recalled from memories (Onuora). This study embeds quotations from participants' interviews throughout the storied accounts to further invite readers into direct conversation with study participants and their stories. Centring Black mothers' narratives in this way is significant because people commonly use storytelling to understand their own experiences and assist others in understanding their experiences (Toliver 513).

Research Context

This chapter draws from data garnered from semi-structured, in-depth interviews with ten Black Canadian mothers. The participant inclusion criteria were as follows:

- women who self-identify as being of Black/African descent living in the Greater Toronto Area;
- women who have engaged in motherwork;
- women who have mothered elementary-aged Black children; and
- women at least eighteen years of age and competent to consent to be interviewed.

I consulted academic and literary pieces written by Black mothers and worked with Black mothers in my personal life to determine the interview questions. I structured the interview as a conversation where I welcomed participants to respond to questions through storytelling. At the beginning of the interview, participants and I explored the possible ways that my research on Black women's motherwork would benefit Black communities and further support Black mother leadership. For example, we discussed how Black mothers sharing and capturing our stories could strengthen solidarity and organizing among Black women. This interview method engaged participants as storytellers and elicited rich, thick descriptions.

Stories shared during interviews captured participants' conceptions of mothering, leadership, and communities of support. The semi-structured, in-depth interview permitted participants to control the flow of conversation and decide which aspects of an issue to emphasize (Banks-Wallace 420). Participants asserted their position as storytellers while I became what JoAnne Banks-Wallace calls the "storytaker" (story listener). The interview provided participants with opportunities to evoke feelings and memories of what it is to be a mother of African descent in Canada across time and space within the research setting. Furthermore, the interview method allowed me to interject and ask clarifying questions. Linda Goss and Marian Barnes remind researchers that such interactions between storyteller and storytaker are common elements of Black story-telling traditions (100). Participants used the interjections to provide clarifying information and ensure the receipt of their message.

Data Analysis

Although stories are the foundation of qualitative research, the development of qualitative methods for data analysis and synthesis grounded in Black storytelling traditions remains largely unexplored by researchers. In *The Substance of Things Hoped for, the Evidence of Things not Seen: Examining an Endarkened Feminist Epistemology*, Cynthia Dillard urges the research community to recognize the validity of Black epistemologies revealed in oral storytelling traditions (664).

Banks-Wallace addresses this call to action by developing a comprehensive analytic process, rooted in diasporic Black storytelling traditions, for collecting and interpreting stories shared during in-depth interviews (Banks-Wallace 410; Banks-Wallace and Parks 81). Banks-Wallace inspired me to reimagine her process in ways that centre the arts in the analysis, synthesis, and presentation of data.

For this study, I used Banks-Wallace's process as a foundation to develop a framework for analyzing and synthesizing research findings into creative nonfiction short stories. This analytic process enabled the study to reveal the depth of participants' lived experiences and how those experiences inform their motherwork and relationships with school officials. The study's method for data analysis included the following:

A. locating the interviews within the historical context and cultural norms;

B. demarcating the boundaries for individual stories;

C. conducting a thematic and functional analysis of stories;

D. grouping stories according to themes and functions;

E. comparing story themes and functions across participant interviews;

F. restructuring participants' memories into storied accounts; and

G. reviewing stories for conspicuous absences and silences.

Locating the Interviews within the Historical Context and Cultural Norms

The social-cultural-political context in which a study is conducted influences story creation, telling, and interpretation (Banks-Wallace 413). As such, I documented directly onto the transcripts references made by participants to specific historical events and cultural conditions, such as the history of Black students in Canadian schools, the West Indian Domestic Scheme (1955) and the Immigration and Refugee Protection Act (2001).

Demarcating the Boundaries for Individual Stories

To analyze the data from the interviews, I established story boundaries consistent with participants' experiences as Black Canadian women. For this study, temporal and spatial boundaries were used as the guides to distinguish one story from another in each interview. These boundaries indicated when the participant talked about an event outside the present context (Livo and Rietz 98). Some keywords included "At the time..."; "What happened was..."; and "Let me tell you about a time...".

Conducting a Thematic and Functional Analysis of Stories

When determining the thematic categories, I honoured participants as thinkers and prioritized key words and phrases they used to tell their stories. Identifying these key words and phrases provided me with insights into the "embodied context of the [story]teller's world" (Banks-Wallace 417). Understanding why specific words and phrases were chosen to describe an event or convey an idea, and how the words were said, was critical in ensuring the correct interpretation of participants' stories (Banks-Wallace 417). Some keywords included gran, granny, and grandma; friend, sister, aunt, and godmother; and take care, help out, and support.

Grouping Stories According to Themes and Functions

Banks-Wallace's process for analyzing stories rooted in Black oral storytelling traditions entails grouping participants' stories into themes. I analyzed each identified story shared by participants in the interviews separately. For each participant, I created a Venn diagram labelled with the thematic categories (i.e., communal mothering, motherline, site of power, and homeplace). These categories were grounded in a Black women's framework, as articulated by Andrea O'Reilly in her book *Toni Morrison and Motherhood: A Politics of the Heart*. I titled each participant's story and grouped them into the thematic categories on the Venn diagram. The Venn diagram allowed me to highlight how a participant's story addressed multiple themes.

Comparing Story Themes and Functions across Participant Interviews

I created a master Venn diagram for the study. Like the participants' Venn diagram, the master Venn diagram was labelled with the thematic categories. I referenced participants' diagrams and plotted the titles of each story collected across interviews onto the master chart. I highlighted emotive stories and addressed the questions guiding the study. I created a chart outlining how each highlighted story connected to the study themes and answered the research questions.

Restructuring Participants' Memories into Storied Accounts

Scholars have written about the role dialogue plays in Black storytelling traditions (Banks-Wallace; Collins; Goss; and Stewart). With the aim to prioritize participants' voices and their relationships with one another, I presented the study's findings as a series of interconnected stories. Each short story began as dialogue. I took direct quotes from the interviews and used creative imagination to order the participants' recalled memories as dialogue. I then used description to reinforce the meaning captured in the dialogue. Description helped me to set participants' stories within a social, political, and historical context. I consulted interview transcripts, and on two occasions, I reconnected with study participants for additional details.

Reviewing Stories for Conspicuous Absences and Silences

I presented the study's findings as a series of interconnected storied accounts. I read the completed short stories aloud and listened for conspicuous absences and silences. I noted directly the openings of the written stories for readers, scholars, and artists to talk back to these silences. I drew on the Black storytelling tradition of call-and-response to elicit audience engagement with study participants. My aim was not to recreate actual Black oral traditions in written form but rather to infuse a sense of orality into the stories. In so doing, the reader, current scholarship, and policy became active contributors in the analysis and synthesis process.

Presentation of Findings as a Creative Nonfiction Story

This article presents the study's findings as an arts-informed research story: *Ay-yai*. In *Ay-Yai*, the footnotes go beyond simply situating participants' stories within scholarship. I included footnotes to capture the many voices, ideas, and structures informing Black maternal life and leadership in Canada. Accordingly, in *Ay-Yai*, footnotes invite readers to participate in an improvised call-and-response where scholarship, audience reflections, and participants' voices are placed in dialogue. The footnotes further situate the story in the historical, political, and social context of participants' everyday lives as Black mothers in Canada. The story's structure invites the reader to consider the ways that multiple research traditions (i.e., storytelling, literary arts, as well as formal qualitative and quantitative scholarly work) come together to reveal Black Canadian mothers' use of storytelling in their leadership practice.

Ay-Yai[1]: Findings as a Creative Non-Fiction Story

Monique, a thirty-four-year-old mother, hunched over her kitchen table and clasped a glass mug. Steam rose from the chamomile tea, circled her nose and grazed her forehead. Mami, a Haitian grandmother, sat across from Monique, her daughter-in-law. The old woman planted her arms on the table. Both the table and the woman were caramel with dark spots and deep grooves. Mami scooped handfuls of cashews from a porcelain bowl into her mouth. Mami's smacking mouth and the wind's howls mixed to create a nighttime soundtrack for the two-story house.

"Sak pase?" Mami wiped her hands in her dress. A trail of salt streaked across the red fabric.

"I'm exhausted, and I have this crick in my neck that won't go away," Monique said to her mother-in-law. She raised the mug to her lips and blew.

"Egypt was such a good girl while you were at the school meeting. She caused no trouble to fall asleep."

"She loves you." Monique sipped her tea and then rested the cup on the table.

"As she should. I'm her grandmother," the Haitian woman giggled. Mami pulled the edges of her headwrap with both hands. The yellow foulard covered her eyebrows and the tips of her ears. The grandmother added, "How was the meeting?"

"The principal and teacher still think Egypt should go to an English school. They say she's struggling with the French,"[2] Monique stated. She twirled the tips of her straight black mane around her index finger. Her diamond wedding ring shimmered under the kitchen light.

"And what do you think?"

"My children's father is Haitian. They deserve to be in a French school as much as any of those little white girls from Quebec,"[3] Monique replied.

"So that settles it. Egypt stays at the school." The old woman grinned.

"I wish the principal, the teachers, and secretaries—shit even the caretakers—would treat me like the white mothers," Monique said. She leaned back into the chair and undid the top two buttons of her mauve silk blouse.

Mami stuffed a fistful of cashews into her mouth.

"Those white mothers have it so easy," Monique continued. "They don't have to argue with teachers and beg the principal to keep their child in the school. They aren't ignored by the secretaries. Even the caretakers ask me if I'm lost when I go to the school. Sometimes, I wish I was a white mom. I'd be so happy."

"You know these white mothers enough to want to be them?" The old woman asked.

Monique gulped her chamomile tea. "No, I guess not. But they're always smiling and laughing with the teachers in the school yard. I want that," Monique said.

"Krik?" Mami asked.

Monique responded, "Krak!"[4]

Mami straightened in her seat and dropped her shoulders. Her voice boomed as she told a Haitian folktale[5]:

One hot day in June, Tonton Bouki[6] *was hard at work in his garden. He dug up yanm and harvested pwa kongo and picked lam veritable. After hours in the field, he decided it was time to quit.*

"I've spent enough time in the garden," Tonton Bouki said. "It's time to make some money at the village market."

He filled a big burlap sack with yams, peas, and breadfruit and set off for the market. In all his haste, Tonton Bouki forgot to eat. When he was halfway to the village, his stomach growled with hunger.

"Oh my, I have to find something to eat," he exclaimed. He walked a little farther and came upon an old woman eating by the side of the road. When Tonton Bouki saw what the old woman was eating, his stomach nearly leapt out of his body. The old woman was relishing her feast, licking her lips and fingers.

"Hello," Tonton Bouki called out. "How are you?"

The old woman didn't respond and continued to eat. You see, the old woman was deaf, so she couldn't hear Tonton Bouki. In fact, she was so focussed on her food she didn't even notice him!

"Please, ma'am," Tonton Bouki stepped closer. "Could you tell me what you are eating?"

Again, the old woman didn't answer, and Tonton Bouki's stomach grumbled. "Please," he begged, "just tell me what you call that fine feast."

It just so happened that right at that moment, the old woman bit down on a pepper so hot that she felt as if her tongue had caught fire. She opened her mouth wide and wailed, "Ay-yai!"

"Thank you!" said Tonton Bouki. "I've never heard of Ay-yai." He smiled and hurried off to the market, determined to buy himself a big bowl of Ay-yai.

At the market, Tonton Bouki quickly sold his yams, peas, and breadfruit. Then, he walked from stall to stall, searching for a bowl of Ay-yai. At each stall, he pulled out his coins and said, "Excuse me, I'd like to buy some Ay-yai." Each time, the vendors laughed and yelled, "You must be mad!"

Everybody laughed at Tonton Bouki and whispered behind his back, and that's how Ti Malice heard the story. When Ti Malice learned that Tonton Bouki was searching for a treat called Ay-yai, he had an idea. He hurried home, ahead of Tonton Bouki, and climbed down to the riverbed. There, he cut some cactus leaves and stuffed them into a burlap bag. Ti Malice placed a few oranges atop the cactus leaves. And on top of these oranges, he put a pineapple. And at the very top, he placed a big potato.

Just before Tonton Bouki arrived home, he saw Ti Malice. "Good day, Tonton Bouki." Ti Malice waved. "And how are you today?"

"I'm dreaming of eating a bowl of Ay-yai," Tonton Bouki said. He asked, "Do you know where I can find some, Ti Malice?" Naturally, Ti Malice said he did. "I just happen to have some Ay-yai in this bag," he said. "Here you go." Tonton Bouki could not believe his luck, and without thinking of all the tricks Ti Malice had played on him in the past, he reached into the sack.

He pulled out the potato. "This isn't Ay-yai," he cried.

"Reach in again," Ti Malice said. So Tonton Bouki did. This time he pulled out the pineapple. "This isn't Ay-yai," he complained, but he reached in again. Next, he brought out the oranges. "And this isn't Ay-yai, Ti Malice. You're making fun of me!"

"I'd never do that," Ti Malice smiled. "Reach in once more. I'm sure you'll be surprised at what you find!" So Tonton Bouki reached in one more time, and this time, he touched the cactus leaves. The sharp needles pierced his hands, and he jumped into the air and cried, "Ay-yai!" Ti Malice grinned. "There you go," he said. "You've found your Ay-yai!"

Between mouthfuls of cashews, Mami warned Monique, "Don't be tricked like Tonton Bouki[7]. He wasted his time thinking that another person's food could satisfy his hunger. Tonton Bouki ran around the market in search of Ay-Yai, when he had all the ingredients in his garden to make a fine feast with his family and friends."

Monique nodded.

The old woman continued, "My daughter, don't spend your time yearning for a white woman's happiness. You are surrounded by Black mothers who have spent lifetimes creating happiness with discarded ingredients. Go cook your feast with other Black women."[8] Mami stuffed the remaining handful of cashews into her mouth.

Story Insights: Black Mother Leadership as the Motherline

In the story *Ay-Yai*, Monique recounts to her mother-in-law, Mami, the hardships she experiences in her relationship with her daughter's principal and kindergarten teacher. The story opens with Monique sitting at the kitchen table with her Haitian mother-in-law, Mami. While detailing the challenges she faces in her relationship with school officials, Monique proclaims to Mami: "I wish I was a white mom." Monique explains to her mother-in-law how anti-Black racism informs her relationships with school personnel and presents obstacles to her daughter enjoying her right to access education in a French language school.

The feelings of frustration and hopelessness that beset Black mothers within the education system culminated with Monique declaring to Mami her desire to be a white mother as "those white mothers have it so easy."

Mami, a member of Monique's community of support, responds by engaging the young mother in a Haitian storytelling ritual. Mami uses the "Krik? Krak!" call-and-response tradition to impart leadership knowledge to Monique. Mami mentors Monique by invoking a Haitian folktale that positions Black mothers as leaders who value working with and learning from other Black mothers to improve their children's schooling experiences.

In the book *Toni Morrison and Motherhood: A Politics of the Heart*, O'Reilly documents Morrison's use of Black feminist/womanist storytelling to theorize a Black motherwork framework. Morrison presents a framework on Black motherwork concerned with the empowerment of Black mothers themselves, their children, and their communities in the face of the racism and sexism that seek to harm them. Toni C. King and S. Alease Ferguson maintain that by "constantly meeting the demands for survival and fending off the noxious stimuli of discrimination, it is altogether possible for Black women to not be cognizant of their own performance as leaders" (5). Although study participants did not use the term "leader" in the interviews, their stories of Black motherwork demonstrate how we, Black mothers, use stories to structure the meaning of our leadership capacities, skills, and approaches in everyday life. King and Ferguson define leadership as "the desire, ability, and efforts to influence the world around us, based upon an ethic of care for self and other and fueled by a vision that one sustains over time" (11). As captured in the story *Ay-Yai*, study participants recast the privileged notion of leadership as one that resides in their Black motherwork and is passed through their stories across generations (Komives and Wagner 50).

O'Reilly asserts the integral role that the motherline plays in Black women's motherwork (52). The motherline centres on communal learning and knowledge systems. In *Ay-Yai*, Mami, like the other participants in the study, draws on Black storytelling traditions to pass on leadership narratives about women's physical, psychological and historical triumphs. Mami uses a Haitian folktale to transmit intergenerational knowledge, values, and worldviews that teach Black mothers and their children self-love, leadership and "an astute opposition to oppression" (King and Ferguson 24).

In the study, participants shared personal accounts, memories, folktales, and adages used by their communities of support to transmit leadership knowledge to one another. King and Ferguson note that adages and folktales shared among Black mothers "prescribe ways [for Black women] to lead and to empower self and the communal network" (11). Study participants valued such cultural narratives and cited them as essential in imparting leadership skills and healing. Through retelling a traditional folktale, Mami used the motherline to create spaces where she and her daughter-in-law could heal each other and themselves from the oppressions inflicted on them by the education system. As such, Mami used storytelling to dismiss the notion that racism, sexism, poverty, and other forms of injustice should be natural, normal, and inevitable parts of everyday Black life (Collins 86). Mami's transmission of intergenerational leadership knowledge through storytelling reestablished Monique as a leader dedicated to working with other Black mothers to resist and undermine oppressive structures steeped in the Canadian education system and beyond.

Call to Action

Black women's maternal stories express our commitment to transforming schools into sites of love, dignity, and justice for our children. The arts-informed research story *Ay-Yai* continued this legacy of Black mothers using stories to articulate and pass on mothering and leadership competencies to other Black women within our networks. This approach to engaging in storytelling provides Black mothers with a method for collecting, writing, analyzing, and theorizing our stories for leadership while also healing from them (Baker-Bell 531). The story *Ay-Yai* leveraged autoethnography, Black women's language and literacy practices, and Black feminist theories to demonstrate Black mothers' use of storytelling to reflect upon, analyze, understand, and communicate our mothering experiences as leadership built on shared learnings passed through the motherline.

As captured in the story *Ay-Yai*, this arts-informed study details the ways that Black women use storytelling, especially folklore, to help plot, map, and collect the archives of Black mothers' leadership in support of their children's, as well as their own, schooling experiences. This arts-informed study demands us to heed the stories of Black mothers, whose leadership experiences are often made invisible within scholarship, and respond to their collective envisioning of just futures for themselves and their children and families within the public education system. I encourage fellow Black thinkers and Black Lives Matter organizers, especially Black mother scholars and leaders, to draw on Black storytelling traditions to provide space for Black mothers to articulate their leadership work. As researchers within the academy and organizers of social movements for Black life, we must continue to give voice to our stories in ways that firmly establish Black mothers as trusted leaders, creators, and theorists.

Endnotes

1. The study explored in this article, as well as the creative non-fiction story *Ay-Yai*, draws from my doctoral dissertation.
2. "Students, teachers, and parents also stated that students were counselled out of intensive French programming if they were struggling" (Sinay et al. 67).
3. "In [French-language] schools the curriculum is taught exclusively in French, with the exception of English language courses. French-language schools in Ontario have a mandate to protect, enhance and transmit the French language and culture" (Ontario Ministry of Education).
4. Krik? Krak! is a Haitian storytelling ritual where the storyteller asks, "Krik?" and the audience responds with "Krak!".
5. "The most respected person in traditional African society was the man or woman who kept the stories. This person, the griot, was the oral historian and educator. The griot was responsible for maintaining the connection between the cultural or historical past and the present" (Banks-Wallace 412).
6. Traditional folktale adapted from Nicolas Beatty's *Uncle Bouki and Ti Malice: A Haitian Folktale*.
7. "Stories become for me the foundation for engaging self and others in the process of reflexivity—focusing the lens and method of inquiry on one's self" (King 89).
8. "Gates (1989) asserted that using stories to ask and answer epistemological and ontological questions in our own voices has played a critical role in the survival of [people of African descent living in the diaspora]" (Banks-Wallace 412).

Works Cited

Aladejebi, Funké O. *"Girl You Better Apply to Teachers' College": The History of Black Women Educators in Ontario, 1940s–1980s.* 2016. York University, PhD dissertation. https://yorkspace.library.yorku.ca/xmlui/bitstream/handle/10315/33442/Aladejebi_Funke_O_2016_PhD.pdf?sequence=2&isAllowed=y. Accessed 24 Dec. 2024.

Baker-Bell, April. "For Loretta: A Black Woman Literacy Scholar's Journey to Prioritizing Self-Preservation and Black Feminist-Womanist Storytelling." *Journal of Literacy Research*, vol. 49, no. 4, 2017, pp. 526–543.

Banks-Wallace, JoAnne. "Talk That Talk: Storytelling and Analysis Rooted in African American Oral Tradition." *Qualitative Health Research*, vol. 12, no. 3, 2002, pp. 410–426.

Banks-Wallace, JoAnne, and Lennette Parks. "So That Our Souls Don't Get Damaged: The Impact of Racism on Maternal Thinking and Practice Related to the Protection of Daughters." *Issues in Mental Health Nursing*, vol. 22, no. 1, 2001, pp. 77–98.

Beatty, Nicholas. *Uncle Bouki and Ti Malice: A Haitian Folktale.* Wordpress, 15 Mar. 2014, https://nicholasbeatty.wordpress.com/2014/03/15/uncle-bouki-and-ti-malice-ahaitian-folktale/. Accessed 24 Dec. 2024.

Cheung, Adrian, and Alexandra Sienkiewicz. "Mississauga Mom Launches Complaint after Police Handcuff her 6-Year-Old Daughter." *CBC/Radio-Canada*, 3 Feb. 2019, https://www.cbc.ca/news/canada/toronto/mississauga-mom-launches-complaint-after-police-handcuff-her-6-year-old-daughter-1.3964827. Accessed 24 Dec. 2024.

Collins, Patricia Hill. *Black Feminist Thought: Knowledge, Consciousness, and the Politics of Empowerment.* Routledge, 2000.

Dei, George, J. Sefa, et al. *Indigenous Knowledges in Global Contexts: Multiple Readings of our World.* University of Toronto Press, 2000.

Dillard, Cynthia B. "The Substance of Things Hoped for, the Evidence of Things Not Seen: Examining an Endarkened Feminist Epistemology in Educational Research and Leadership." *Qualitative Studies in Education*, vol. 13, 2000, pp. 661–81.

Fearon, Stephanie. *For Our Children: Black Motherwork and Schooling.* 2020. University of Toronto, dissertation, https://tspace.library.utoronto.ca/handle/1807/103353. Accessed 24 Dec. 2024.

Goss, Linda, and Clay Goss. *Jump Up and Say!: A Collection of Black Storytelling*. Simon & Schuster, 1995.

Goss, Linda, and Marian E. Barnes. *Talk That Talk: An Anthology of African-American Storytelling*. Simon & Schuster, 1998.

James, Carl, et. al. *Race and Well-Being: The Lives, Hopes, and Activism of African Canadians*. Fernwood Publishing, 2010.

King, Toni C., and S. Alease Ferguson. *Black Womanist Leadership: Tracing the Motherline*. State University of New York Press, 2011.

Komives, Susan R., and Wendy Wagner. *Leadership for a Better World: Understanding the Social Change Model of Leadership Development*. Jossey-Bass, 2017.

Konguavi, Thandiwe. "School Board Lifts Ban on Mother in Do-Rag Feud, Denies Conduct was Racially Motivated." *CBC/Radio-Canada*, 17 Dec. 2019, https://www.cbc.ca/news/canada/edmonton/school-board-lifts-ban-on-mother-in-dorag-feud-1.5400150. Accessed 24 Dec. 2024.

Livo, Norma, and Sandra Rietz. *Storytelling: Process and Practice*. Libraries Unlimited, 1986.

Maynard, Robyn. *Policing Black Lives: State Violence in Canada from Slavery to the Present*. Fernwood Publishing, 2017.

McGarvey, Dan. "Few Details Offered on CBE School Bullying Review as Another Calgary Mother Calls for Action." *CBC/Radio-Canada*, 21 May 2019, https://www.cbc.ca/news/canada/calgary/cbe-calgary-bullying-schools-1.5142536. Accessed 24 Dec. 2024.

Morrison, Toni. "The Site of Memory." *Inventing the Truth: The Art and Craft of Memoir*. Edited by W. Zinsser. Houghton Miffin, 1987, pp. 103–124.

Ontario Ministry of Education. *French-Language Education in Ontario*. Ontario Ministry of Education. 2019, http://www.edu.gov.on.ca/eng/amenagement/. Accessed 24 Dec. 2024.

Onuora, Adwoa Ntozake. *Anansesem: Telling stories and storytelling African maternal pedagogies*. Demeter Press, 2015.

O'Reilly, Andrea. *Toni Morrison and Motherhood: A Politics of the Heart*. State University of New York Press, 2004.

REDE4 Black Lives. "Research, Evaluation, Data, Ethics." *The Call for a Protocol Our Process*, https://rede4blacklives.com/the-protocol/. Accessed 24 Dec. 2024.

Reddekopp, Lorenda. "Toronto Police Officer Charged After Man, 19, Beaten and Blinded in Left Eye." *CBC/Radio-Canada*, 18 July 2017, https://www.cbc.ca/news/canada/toronto/siu-charges-toronto-police-officer-1.4209353. Accessed 24 Dec. 2024.

Smitherman, Geneva. *Talkin and Testifyin: The Language of Black America*. Wayne State University Press, 1977.

Sinay, Erhan, et. al. *Toronto District School Board French as a Second Language Program Review: Developmental Evaluation (Research Report No. 18/19-03)*. *Toronto District School Board*, 8 March 20219, https://www.tdsb.on.ca/Portals/0/docs/TDSB%20French%20Programs%20Review%20Mar082019.pdf. Accessed 24 Dec. 2024.

Stewart, Carlyle. *Soul Survivors: An African American Spirituality*. Westminster John Knox Press, 1997.

Toliver, Stephanie R. "Can I Get a Witness? Speculative Fiction as Testimony and Counterstory." *Journal of Literacy Research*, vol. 52, no. 4, 2020, pp. 507–29.

10.

Does Anyone Else Care? Black Mothering in the Time of COVID-19 and Black Lives Matter

Chelsi West Ohueri

"Okay well let me get out of here," our babysitter tells us, as she collects her things and ushers her eight-year-old daughter towards the door. She is not just our weekly babysitter but also my oldest daughter's teacher. But because of the pandemic and ongoing quarantine, she was recently indefinitely furloughed along with every other teacher at the early childhood centre. It was June 2020—up to this point my spouse and I had been juggling our two kids at home as best as we could; I performed most of the childcare duties, since the semester had ended, and my work as a professor was considered more flexible for the summer. I struggled significantly with my research and writing—they had become nonexistent. My days had become consumed with Kinetic Sand, *Ada Twist Scientist*, and *PBS Kids*. I was behind on several deadlines, spending late-night hours writing and submitting what I could and sending apologetic emails for what I could not. Once the girls' school announced that it was officially furloughing teachers for the foreseeable future, I messaged ours to see how she was doing and to gauge whether she felt comfortable watching my kids for a few hours a day. At that time, we did not have physical contact with anyone outside of distant waves to grandparents from inside our car, and we were willing to agree with her to continue limited interactions for everyone's health and safety. We told her we would pay whatever rate she desired and informed her that she could bring her daughter. We even encouraged it, as we knew how much our girls liked playing with her.

"I have to head out now," she said. "I'm going to drop off food at my parents' house." She explained that her mother was not feeling well and that it was not COVID-19 related but rather an ongoing health issue. Her parents were getting up there in years, as my grandmother would say, and our teacher-sitter was their primary caretaker. COVID-19 had of course reshaped their relationship, as she could no longer make frequent quality visits due to their underlying health conditions. "And after I leave their house," she continued, "I have to have a virtual meeting with my nephew's doctor." She went on to explain that after her sister passed away years ago, she became the legal guardian for her three nieces and nephews. One nephew was also experiencing health challenges, so she had to meet with his doctor about an action plan. It was not until this moment that I fully comprehended the extent of her care-work—how she managed to care for her daughter, her parents, her nephew, and my kids. She did it all with so much grace and poise, conducting science experiments with our oldest and rocking my youngest to sleep, sweetly lulling her with songs.

Black women are providers. They provide for their children, families, neighbourhoods, and community. I am a Black woman, mother, daughter, granddaughter, and niece, emerging from and connected to a long line of Black women who have cared for those who could not or would not care for themselves. My pandemic nights are filled with reflections about the carework that Black women do. We do the work of mending, tending, and lending, often giving of ourselves to the point of depletion. Black women are disproportionately represented among essential workers. Those of us who are teachers provide so much care for our students. Black women arrange meals for grieving families and lead prayer circles. Black women provide care and backup care and plan Zoom funerals and wakes with limited attendees while organizing rallies, marches, and movements against anti-Blackness. While health officials issue mandates to shelter-in-place, Black mothers provide that shelter in and outside of their homes as they care for those around them.

Shortly after our teacher-sitter leaves, I load the kids in the car, hoping they will both take naps while I run errands. By now, in season two of the pandemic, I have learned more tactics for completing tasks with as little human interaction as possible. It starts to rain as we make our way to the grocery store pickup line and then to the pharmacy. It is a specialized clinic pharmacy that exclusively treats people with cancer and sickle cell disease. Except for patients, they do not allow anyone inside, and the person on the phone has reiterated that the clinic is operating with extreme caution. I park in the designated space and open the back of my car, careful not to wake the children. A representative from the pharmacy comes to the car, carefully places the medicine in the back, and then gives me a thumbs up so that I can get back out to close the hatch door. The girls and I begin our thirty-minute drive north to my sister-in-law's house. I leave the sickle cell medication on the front porch along with a bag of fruit and some Lysol wipes I remarkably snagged the previous week. I text her once I am back at the car to let her know everything is outside, and I watch as she opens the door, waving to me from afar and mouthing, "Thank you."

Several hours later, I am sitting in my rocking chair. It is just before midnight, and I am nursing my toddler. At eighteen months, I thought she would have weaned by now, but her grip on me is strong, and my eyes are too heavy to consider another option for soothing her back to sleep. Like many others at this moment, I am having trouble sleeping because the news preoccupies me, and I feel anxious about mothering Black children. Nighttime is also the time when I can play catch-up on work. Sleep is luring me, but I know it is a trick. The sleep is not consistent, continual, or comfortable. I scroll through my email inbox. There are several messages from my students who want to talk about COVID-19, whiteness and anti-mask rallies, and Black Lives Matter protests. I have recently taught courses on white nationalism and health inequality, so it makes sense that they want to dialogue. I agree to arrange a time the following week during my kids' naptime for us to convene an informal Zoom talk session to discuss the current sociopolitical landscape. I know they want to vent and ask questions. They are a good group of students who are eager to learn. But I also know they are also looking for ways to cope and somehow help; they are searching for answers—answers that I too am seeking.

There are other emails from my relatives about what was supposed to be our upcoming family reunion. COVID-19 has stolen this from us. We could not meet the previous year due to a hurricane threat, and the reunion occurs every other year, so this will now make two years since we have gathered. I feel I have let my grandma down. She was the driving force behind the reunions, which date back to the mid-1970s. They were called the Centerville Family Reunion back then because both of my paternal grandparents were from that area and large families. My grandmother was one of thirteen, and we have often joked that the tiny town of Centerville, Texas only consists of our kinfolk. I take so much pride in the reunion, but I also carry a fear that I am not meeting the mark as an organizer. My grandmother laboured tirelessly to pull off extraordinary and memorable celebrations, with the torch eventually passing to my older cousins and my father after she passed. Now the torch has landed with my generation, and I regularly worry about falling short. I sigh deeply. I know we cannot safely gather this year—hell, we are all sheltering in place and most hotels have cancelled reservations. I know people miss seeing one another. The reunion is a time when we unite young and old and when we simply enjoy being together. I sigh again. My daughter's eyes are beginning to close as she settles closer to my chest. I feel myself slowly beginning to dream with her.

I am jolted awake by my four-year-old who is shaking my left shoulder. She says she is scared and needs to cuddle because of a frightening dream. Still holding my toddler, I delicately stand up from the recliner and take her to her crib. I pull my oldest daughter to my hip and take her back to the chair. She rests her head on my shoulder. I look at the time: 1:13 a.m. As we rock in the chair, I think about Aiyana Stanley-Jones. Her story comes to me often, especially in the middle of the night: a seven-year-old Black girl, a precious baby, who was killed by police as she slept next to her grandmother. It was just after midnight when officers released a flash grenade and began shooting into her home, where they claimed they were looking for a suspect in a murder investigation. Officer Joseph Weekly fired the shot that struck and killed Aiyana. He claimed that her grandmother had grabbed his gun, which is why he shot back, but her grandmother and neighbours said that never happened. Evidence from Officer Weekly's trial later revealed that there were no fingerprints from Aiyana's grandmother on the gun, and no one corroborated Weekly's version of events. I think about Aiyana's grandmother's testimony during the trial, as she cried out, her wails of agony and anguish piercing the air: "Why you do it?" she demanded. "Please tell me. Why you come in my house like that.... She was only a baby, a baby! I get NO sleep!" she yelled. "The flashbacks—I wouldn't wish them on nobody in the world, not even you," she said to Officer Weekly as she was escorted out of the courtroom. The judge claimed that such outbursts were not permitted, but perhaps the weight of the guilt was too much to bear because the hands of the entire Detroit justice system were stained with the blood of injustice. Black mothers, grandmothers, sisters, aunties, play aunties and cousins, and godmothers work so hard to provide care, sustain shelter, and make homes for their families. But as the lives of Breonna Taylor, Sophia Cook, Atatiana Jefferson, Regis Korchinski-Paquet, and Aiyana Stanley-Jones show, Black women are not safe from state violence, even at home.

I think about the news stories I have listened to throughout the day. My pre-COVID-19 work commute often provided moments of refuge, a way of dealing with the ups and downs of day-to-day life. Now talk radio and podcasts have become my shelter-in-place soundtrack, with me catching kernels of information whenever I can. I listen as NPR commenters report about police officers killing unarmed Black people, providing listeners with details about the officers' lives outside of the police force, their families, and their kids. Perhaps the victims' lives are sometimes talked about in this same way, but I long for more coverage about the shattering of Black families and of mothers losing their children. I do not want shows that amplify the agony or create a spectacle of trauma. I yearn for something more real—stories that humanize Black victims and mothers and authentically force audiences to reckon with pain and despair. I do not want to hear about the disruptions to the officers' lives and jobs. I want shows emphasizing the inescapable heaviness of these losses and truly elucidating the anguish. That anguish haunts the minds of Black mothers who have lost their babies, infusing the worries of those mothers who know their children have to stare down an anti-Black world every single day.

My thinking has become increasingly anxious. My older daughter is asleep again, but I am now afraid to put her back in her bed. I want to keep her close, but I also want to stretch out in my bed. I eventually decide to take her to her room. It is 2:30 a.m. My alarm will go off in three and a half hours, and I am sure my Fitbit will once again measure my sleep as poor. Since the start of the pandemic, I have read many thought pieces for mothers and about mothering: ways to entertain kids, fun crafts to keep your toddlers busy, and ways to prioritize self-care.

They all ring hollow, and the notion of self-care always causes me to smirk. I am tired, overwhelmed, and stressed. At this exact moment, I am all cared out. I get downstairs and slump into my bed. I am screaming into the metaphoric void, and I wonder if anyone even cares.

11.

Thank God for Aunties

Devynity

For my Aunt Carole and the Barbaras and Sharons and Marys and Alices and Maraldas that love love love

Not quite like mommies

Thank God for these women

That nurture my existence

That point

Me in the right direction

They make they're point

They be on point

And always an ear one can confide in

      Hook a plate up!

So inviting

Provide true perspective

From an angle that was never seen

Til auntie lifted up her manicured finger and pointed it out

And ain't even make me feel no way about pointing it out

That's love. No doubt

Gotta love Aunties

With uncles as complements

Common sense

confidence

Thank you God for Aunties

The ones that are of blood and the ones that come from kinship

Kisses on my cheek

She'd leave a certain shade of lipstick

Sway her hips with extra shift

Usher me in the pew sideways for Sunday service singing the hymn she knew by heart

All the parts

Assisted in the production that was my upbringing

And another shining example I have to reference in the making of this life I'm leading as the woman I am striving to become

Thank God for Aunties

With bomb mac and cheese recipes

Hair-braiding technique

Head between

lotioned knees

Butt on pillow/Still gonna be sore in the middle when I get up

Tender-headed child's nightmare

But every braid was considerate of my pain

Firm when its necessary
      your words be understood

Thank God for Aunties

12.

The Light We Carry: An Interview with Photographer Heather Lynch

Haile Eshe Cole

Haile: So how did you get into photography? Why is photography your chosen medium for storytelling?

Heather: In many ways, I feel like photography chose me. My earliest memory of holding a camera was at age seven. Around that time, my mother had been misdiagnosed for months, and the day the doctors finally diagnosed her condition, they told her she had stage-four breast cancer and how long she had to live. Looking back, I realize that from that day forward, she began preparing my family and me for her transition. She had me take countless photos and videos of her singing, cooking, and modelling. Through those moments behind the camera, I developed a deep admiration for the camera. After my mother's passing, like many kids, I grew out of my childhood hobbies. But in high school, I discovered a passion for documentary filmmaking. After graduating during the pandemic, I even pursued a film and TV program at my community college. However, the program leaned heavily towards live television production, and I felt uninspired. Everything changed when I walked into the International Center of Photography (ICP). Seeing the photo books there altered my perspective entirely. For the first time, I understood the power of visual art in shaping how we see ourselves and the world around us. That experience reconnected me to my younger self, and it felt like things began to align. I truly believe that my struggles with school were part of my sanctification process; now I can see how this was God moulding and preparing me to step into the assignment He had over my life from this point on. That same day, I asked if ICP was hiring, and I ended up getting a job there. I began taking classes, immersing myself in the art of visual storytelling. As I became more familiar with the craft, I started developing my own visual language, and everything began to fall into place. I believe God led me to photography because it is my gift and my calling. It's the medium through which I'm able to express myself while uplifting and amplifying underrepresented stories.

Haile: That's an amazing story. I appreciate you sharing that. So then for this project, *The Light We Carry,* what inspired you to do this project, and what does it mean to you?

Heather: The inspiration for the project *The Light We Carry* came from being deeply influenced by the women in my family, especially my grandmother and my aunts. After my mom passed, I would visit my family over summer to spend time with my cousins but oftentimes as my little cousins played. I would sit with my aunts as they discussed their lives, decisions, and challenges. These conversations offered me profound insight into how they navigated adversity, often with grace and resilience. I've always been that niece who was eager to understand, always soaking up their wisdom. I was never anyone's daughter—I was their niece, and that gave me a unique vantage point. This upbringing shaped me into an old soul, with a deep admiration for the strength and perseverance of these women.

During my adolescence, I was exposed to media and television that perpetuated the negative stereotypes of Black people from reality TV shows like *Bad Girls Club, Basketball Wives,* and *Love & Hip-Hop* and certain hip-hop music videos to even the news—watching Black people be targeted and oppressed just because of their identity. This imagery dominated the media landscape, and as a young Black girl, I felt unseen and misunderstood because I didn't resonate with the lifestyles they portrayed. Even though I didn't see these behaviours portrayed through my family, I realized how these learned behaviours showed up in the ways I interacted with my peers. This disconnect began to affect me. I started acting out in school. I remember getting a drink thrown at me during my freshman year of high school in the cafeteria, which led to a fight. It wasn't until later that I realized we were mimicking some of the behaviour we had absorbed from television—gossiping, fighting, and thriving on conflict. After transferring to a school in Manhattan and connecting with friends from diverse backgrounds, I began to see the deeper implications of my identity as a Black woman. The stories told about us weren't just inaccurate—they were damaging. Crafted by people outside our culture, these portrayals didn't glorify our truths or celebrate our complexities; instead, they erased them. I felt the weight of having to overly prove myself in spaces that were never designed for me to thrive. It became clear that I couldn't wait for others to tell our stories with the care and depth they deserved—I had to create my own lane.

Haile: You talked about photographing women in your family and how they see themselves. Do you think that seeing the photos that you have taken of them changed their perspectives of how they see themselves?

Heather: Yes! I showed the photos to my grandmother and my aunts, and they absolutely loved them. My grandmother, who's eighty-three, was especially moved. She said, "This is the last photo I ever need to take." She's healthy and doing well, but I think at her age thoughts like that naturally come up. She even mentioned that this would be the photo she'd want people to remember her by—her memorial photo at her funeral. It was the first time I've seen her so excited about seeing herself. That moment was powerful because it showed me how meaningful it is to portray someone in a way that celebrates their essence and allows them to see themselves with pride and joy.

Haile: You shared previously some of the stereotypes of Black women and the caricatures of them. How do you feel like your work combats that?

Heather: I think my work embodies the essence of a woman showing up fully in her femininity, free from the stereotypes that have historically been imposed on her. When I photograph Black women, my goal is to portray them as I see them—multifaceted, powerful, and deeply human. It's my way of countering the narrow portrayals we often see in the media, where Black women are reduced to being "baby mothers," fighting over men, or struggling with addiction.

Yes, these realities exist within our community, as they do in others, but they are not the sum of who we are. These stereotypes perpetuate a mental block, limiting not only how others see us but also how we see ourselves. My work is about proper representation—showing the dignity, grace, and complexity of Black women that so often go unseen. It's a reminder that we are more than caricatures: we are creators, nurturers, leaders, and dreamers.

Through my lens, I aim to tell a story that uplifts and affirms. It's not about denying the challenges we face, but about expanding the narrative to reflect the richness of our experiences and the limitless potential we hold.

Haile: Your work is currently being shown at ICP. So it's one thing to consider what you want other Black women to see when they see your work. But is there anything? When someone comes to look at your photography, what do you want them to get out of it or take away from it? If anything?

Heather: When someone views my work, I want them to gain a fresh perspective. Even within our communities, we're often conditioned to internalize harmful stereotypes—that Black people are aggressive, unintelligent, or incapable of expressing emotions in healthy ways. These narratives are designed to oppress us, and through my work, I aim to challenge them. I want people to see the rawness of my expression: my unique perspective as a young Black woman sharing what Blackness means to me. More than anything, I want people to see themselves in my work—to find their own experiences reflected in it. I hope it conveys just how much we matter because we do.

Growing up, my mother had brain cancer, and I vividly remember how people would look at her. She had staples in her head and looked visibly unwell, yet some people seemed to lack the compassion to see her humanity. They didn't know her story, but their stares carried assumptions, shaped by stereotypes. That experience changed me. It made me want to create art that allows others to see us as I see us—with empathy, depth, and dignity.

I wanted to use this opportunity to have my first exhibition in a museum to jumpstart my life's work: reclaiming narratives, challenging the misrepresentation of marginalized communities, and authentically portraying those who often go unseen and underappreciated. I had the privilege of working at ICP while this exhibition was on display, allowing me to engage with visitors from all walks of life. These interactions have reinforced the transformative power of art. This work has not only sparked meaningful change in the perspectives of non-Black audiences but has also served as a source of inspiration and empowerment for Black women navigating a world that too often undervalues their worth.

Haile: I love that. So then for the book, you've already used the language about us mattering. But for this book around motherhood and Black Lives Matter, what made you feel your work would fit this theme?

Heather: My work fits seamlessly with the theme of this book because it is fundamentally about honouring Black women, particularly through the lens of motherhood and resilience. *The Light We Carry* aligns with mothering and motherwork because both are deeply personal explorations of family lineage and the enduring strength of matriarchal figures. By portraying the experiences of Black mothers, my work sheds light on their often overlooked but vital roles in our lives and communities.

Photography has a unique ability to convey emotions and stories in a way that's both digestible and impactful. It offers a visual narrative that speaks volumes in a single still, creating a lasting impression. For me, portraying Black women in a regal and authentic light is not just about representation—it's about celebration and reclamation. I see this opportunity as divinely aligned with my life's work and a powerful platform to continue reclaiming narratives and affirming the dignity and value of Black women.

Haile: I love that. Hearing you talk, I'm super inspired. You almost made me cry when I was listening to you. I just feel like what you're doing is super powerful. Your work is beautiful and thank you. You're a young sister. You have so much time to grow, and it is just really exciting.

Heather: Thank you so much. I really appreciate you.

Artist Statement

Through this body of work, I seek to honor the legacy of the remarkable women in my family, the pillars whose contributions often go unnoticed in the broader societal narrative. It is a celebration of their resilience, their sacrifices, and their unwavering love, a testament to the enduring spirit of Black women and the transformative power of familial love. Which has shaped me into the woman I am today. Through portraiture and storytelling, I invite viewers to reevaluate preconceived notions and perceptions, to recognize the invaluable role these women play in shaping our communities and our lives. It is my hope that this body of work will serve as both a tribute to their legacy and a catalyst for greater understanding and appreciation. *The Light We Carry* is a testament to the indomitable spirit of the matriarchs who have illuminated my path, and a reminder of the profound impact of love, resilience, and family.

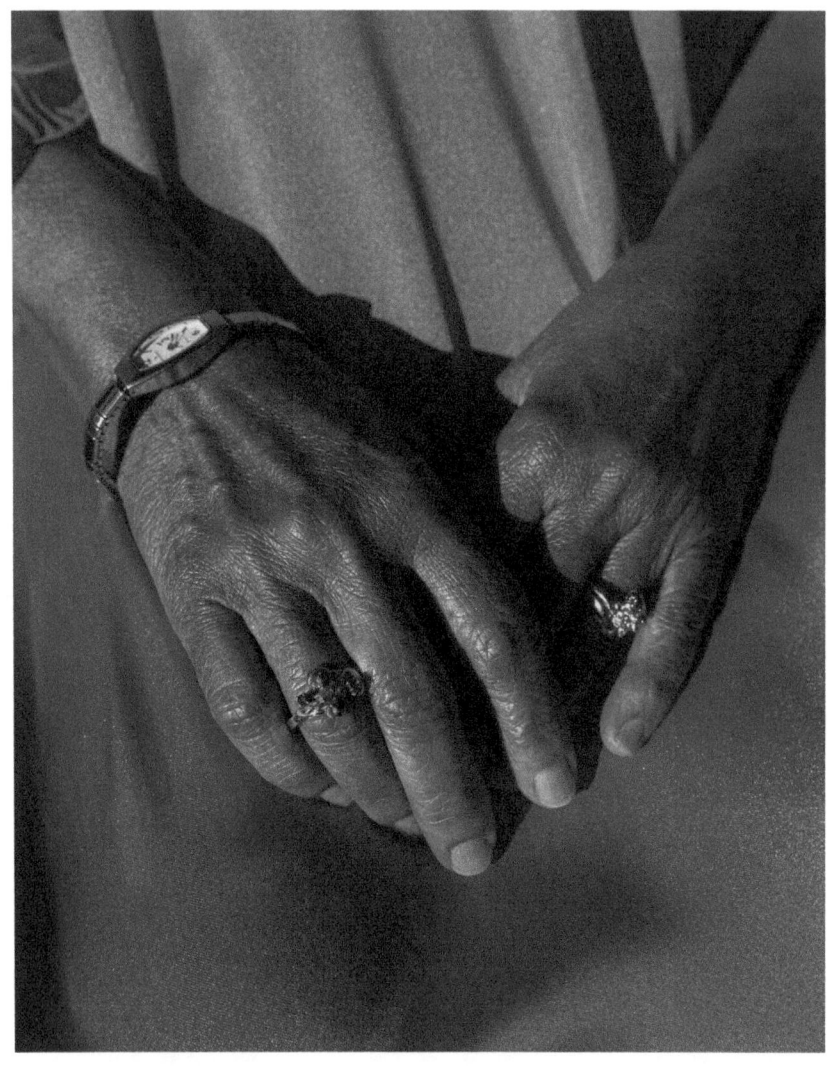

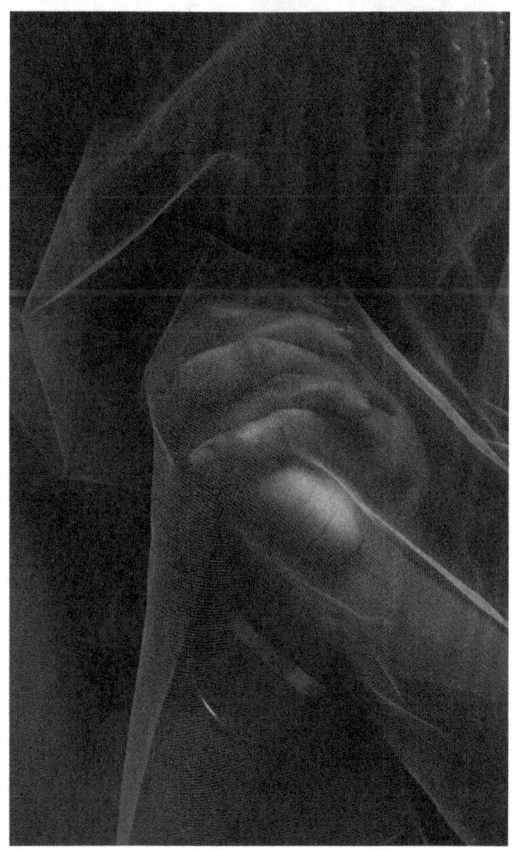

In Loving Memory of my mother Dona.
Though you are no longer with us, you will never be forgotten. May your memory be forever held in the pages of this book.

For more of Heather Lynch's work, scan the QR code.

13.

For You, Infinitely

Adriel Michelle Barnett

Artist Statement

My practice explores identity, heritage, and belonging within the Afro-Caribbean diaspora, weaving together the mythology of family stories and cultural memory. Through my work, I aim to bridge generations and connect the past and present in a dialogue honouring the resilience, ingenuity, and enduring spirit of my ancestors.

Through the lens of personal family history, I explore themes of survival, strength, and enduring familial love while honouring the ingenuity and traditions that sustained enslaved Africans. I merge archival photos with my contemporary imagery and am motivated to create a dialogue bridging past and present generations through shared stories. I emphasize the continuity and deep-rooted connections within the Afro-Caribbean diaspora by connecting these generations. My art celebrates the resilience and spirit of the diaspora and affirms identity and unity across time and space.

My mother's journey from St. Thomas, Jamaica to Brooklyn, New York marks the beginning of the narrative in my work—the complex interplay of heritage, personal history, and the shifting landscapes of home and belonging. My process is rooted in decontextualizing and reconstructing images. I blend my photographs with archival images, particularly those from the cherished pages of her childhood photo album. In these reconstructions, I evoke a sense of nostalgia and pay homage to the past while creating something new.

Project Statement

For You, Infinitely invites viewers to listen to the stories of past and present, connecting generations across time and space. Rooted in the cherished pages of my mother Nicoli's childhood photo album, this project explores her life in St. Thomas, Jamaica, and her migration to Brooklyn, New York as a young adult. Each faded page reveals the history of my family's dreams, love, and resilience.

By juxtaposing contemporary imagery with archives from my mother's childhood, I illuminate a narrative of resilience and perseverance. An affinity is forged as my nieces lean into the whispers of stories, bridging generations to feel the transmission of heritage. This intergenerational act tying my mother and my nieces transcends mere physical interaction. It becomes a lyrical dialogue across time, where memories flow like a river through the ages.

Reflecting on the intimate bonds between family, my work asks viewers to consider how these connections shape our identities. In my practice combined with ground provisions such as breadfruit, pumpkin, and more, pays homage to the ingenuity and strength of our ancestors. Historically, ground provisions, known as root vegetables, played a crucial role in sustaining enslaved Africans in Jamaica, who cultivated them to maintain survival and a connection to their agricultural traditions despite oppressive conditions.

For You, Infinitely is a tribute to the resilience of my family and the broader Afro-Caribbean diaspora. It seeks to illuminate the enduring spirit that sustains us, transcending time and space to affirm our place in the world and our connection to one another.

FOR YOU, INFINITELY

FOR YOU, INFINITELY

For more of Adriel Michelle Barnett's work, scan the QR code.

Section III

Violence and Trauma: "Rinsing Pain and Casting Wishes"

14.

Almost Human

Haile Eshe Cole

Artist Statement

Haile's creative body of work centres on the lived experiences of people. Broadly conceived, her work explores the humanity in Black life—unveiling its beauty in the mundane. It is preoccupied with various manifestations of Black love and care for self and community and often manifests in representations of Black women, children, and families. Haile uses portraiture and documentary photography to tell compelling visual stories. In this way, she can beautifully meld her community work with her anthropology background and creative passion for photography. She believes that the process of image making and artistic creation is inherently liberating and hopes that her work will contribute to the transformative work of writing new self-determined narratives. Her goal is to create timeless images that tell impactful stories, touch people's hearts, and serve as a snapshot of the human experience and the beauty of the human soul and essence.

15.

Conto De Cantos Chorados (A Tale of Crying Songs): A Single Mother's Experience

Cynthia Rachel Esperança

Maria is a Black mother who bravely faces the atrocities of the world to raise her four children: Paulo, Pedro, Alex, and Júlio. She raises Black boys within a society that does not support Black bodies. This story tells about the life of Maria and her children, but it could be the story of any Black mother who needs to care, love, and protect her children. Things don't always go as planned; the path of raising Black children goes far beyond what their mothers want for them. The story of Maria, Paulo, Pedro, Alex, and Júlio speaks much about this: She is a mother who protects, feeds, cares, and loves but who, at a certain moment, finds herself unaware of her affection. Life takes other directions, which no mother wants for her sons and daughters.

The story told here would easily fit not only in the mouths of women but in various experiences of Black women who carry with them children abandoned by their fathers. Maria raised all her children by herself. A Black woman, she had always understood what paternal abandonment was. One day, Maria looked at her four boys. She didn't even know what to do with them. With a sigh, Maria blurted, "I'm glad you have me." The boys stayed there in an act of complicity with their mother, even without knowing what was happening to her.

Every day, Maria left home and worked hard to support the four boys. "This girl's hard life," people on the street commented. But Maria did not let herself be discouraged.

After a full day of work, she would always sit on the floor, call the four of them, and ask, "What did you do in my absence?" The four of them looked at each other, and between looks, Paulo, the oldest, always started talking.

"Mom, we really stayed at home. I tidied the bathroom, Pedro washed the dishes, Alex swept the door, and Júlio watched cartoons all day."

"Seriously?" asked the mother.

"We're telling the truth, Mom."

Maria stayed there longer, listening to the stories of her children's day. Afterwards, Maria, who had no one to help her with things around the house, prepared dinner for her children. The four of them sat in the small space of the room. As Maria prepared the food, she heard the boys whispering, "I'm going to tell my mother everything." The mother then pricked up her ears to understand what all the fuss was about.

The mother then realized that no matter how much she had always built a space of trust with her children, they were already starting to keep their secrets. And she stood there, with the wooden spoon in her hand, thinking about what it would be like to leave the house every day to go to work and leave the four Black boys and their secrets at home. Even without verbalizing it, Maria missed someone who could play with her on this team. That she could, somehow, not let these Black boys struggle in life. There were minutes of listening that seemed eternal to the mother's ears. She no longer knew whether to interrupt the conversation, finish cooking, sit in the corner, or just cry—and the four of them there, in a game of who would deliver whom.

The next day, Maria, before even leaving the house, took the two biggest ones, leaned them against the wall, and said, "You are my eyes inside this house; if anything happens in my absence, trust will be gone." The boys looked at each other, but Maria had to go to work, and they stayed there, disregarding everything their mother said.

Paulo, the eldest, went to stay with the community boys. He walked the streets all day long. Pedro, the second oldest, was getting involved with other boys in the community carrying out petty thefts in the neighbourhood below. Alex, the third youngest, no longer attended school. The brothers would pack him up and leave him at the school entrance, and as his older brothers didn't wait for him to enter, the little one would turn around and do other favours at the market door on the same street as the school. Julio, the baby, stayed with the alcoholic neighbour. Maria didn't know any of this.

Maria left the house to make sure her children had everything they needed. Poor Maria. She no longer had much control over everything that was going on in the kids' lives. And it wasn't a lack of love; it wasn't the mother's absence. It was a childish thing that was difficult to control at the age of curiosity.

Maria was unhappy at work. She walked back and forth, picking up the phone to call her neighbours now and then. She tried to create a protection net for her boys on several occasions. These networks are where women in the community are as much mothers of other children as they are of their own.

And the neighbours always said:

"Maria, I didn't see anyone dressed up for school…"

"Maria, I saw Alex at the market door in his school uniform…"

"Maria…"

There were endless complaints. But what could Maria do? What could a Black mother who needed to work to support her children do? It was a Friday when Maria decided to leave work early and surprise them at home. She went to the market, bought biscuits, yogurt, chocolate, and the pasta that the boys liked, and went home to make the boys, her boys, happy.

On the way up the favela, the residents were already alerting Maria to what was happening. As she climbed the stairs, the other boys helped Maria in the community, and the mothers updated Maria on the events. She heard everything. But for her the boys were at home, at school, except running around causing trouble. The love for her children sometimes blinded the mother.

When she got home, there was silence. Maria looked around and didn't see anyone, not even the baby. She organized the purchases and took a shower. She made the pasta just the way her children liked it. She didn't even turn on the TV. She just sat on the sofa and waited.

Maria arrived home at 2:50 p.m. and sat on the sofa at 4:07 p.m. It was almost 7:00 p.m., and Maria was there, sitting, waiting. Sometimes, she asked God, Oxalá, and the goddesses so that her children would arrive home safely. Maria, the mother of four Black boys, disappeared between the sofa and the window. She wasn't even breathing properly; she was waiting. Around 7:52 p.m., the boys arrived little by little, running. The first was Alex, who was dirty and smelly after spending the whole day on the street. He went straight to the bathroom, not even noticing his mother's presence, who stayed quiet on the couch. Shouting, Paulo, the eldest, who was carrying Júlio in his arms, entered the house. When he saw his mother sitting on the sofa, the boy turned pale, his eyes wide. Júlio ran into his mother's arms.

At 8:00 p.m., the siege was already closed. The boys didn't even have anything to say to this mother, and she didn't even say anything either. She just looked. In this mother's head, there was a tangle of bad things going on. Julio was on the floor with the few toys his mother could give him. Alex couldn't even look at his mother. Paulo didn't even sit down, and Pedro didn't arrive.

Silence took over the shack. Now, at the height of her concern, the mother paced back and forth without saying a word. It was late, almost 10:00 pm; the mother's feelings at that point were already mixed between despair, sadness, and anger. The boys who were at home napped on the sofa; Paulo tried a few times to talk to his mother.

Maria then sat in front of her son, looked into his eyes, and collapsed. Maria, the mother of four Black boys, broke down. She was stripped of her strength, fragile before her eldest son. Maria cried. She sobbed and spoke. Quietly, almost hoarsely, Maria said: "I don't know when this all started. But I'm broken. Shattered. I only have you and you me. I talk to you about everything. I trusted you. And look how you repay me... Why? Did I fail? Wasn't I a good mother? Tell me."

Paulo couldn't say anything. Upon seeing his mother's despair, the boy just cried. He began to understand the gravity of everything they were doing behind his mother's back. Desperately, he tried to console his mother. He suggested that the two of them go look for Pedro. After all, he knew where his brother was and who he hung out with. Maria left the house. She called the women and men of the community and asked them to help search for her son. The community was in solidarity with the mother. A friend stayed at home to watch the sleeping boys. Around thirteen people went down the hill to look for Pedro, and many were on alert in the local alleys, waiting for the boy. They walked a lot. Everywhere. They spoke to passersby. At that point, a few people were walking on the street. Paulo saw a man who lived in a carriage and ran to ask about his brother's whereabouts. The man was a little drunk, so a group gathered around him to ask about the boy.

A little dizzy, the man narrated the facts. There had been an attempted robbery, followed by a dragnet involving many boys from some local communities and Pedro. Amid the confusion, the establishment's security guards, responsible for bringing order, caught several boys. Maria listened to the facts in tears.

The old man tried to doze off, but the residents didn't let him; they wanted to know if he knew anything else. Then he started saying slowly... "They caught them and beat them up." Paulo realized the gravity of everything at this moment. The boy's face changed. Maria fainted. A friendly resident took Maria in his arms and ran with her. Others stayed there to understand the story.

Finally, the old man said, "I heard, but I don't want to get involved in this; they took them to the dump." The residents were stunned, in shock. They returned to the community. Paulo together. They sat with him and, like in a village in a quilombo, they hugged him, gave him advice, and made themselves available to help him at all times. But they told him about the responsibility he had as an older brother, who should help his struggling mother. Paulo just listened and cried.

At the hospital, Maria was taking medication intravenously. Her speech didn't make sense. In her delirium, Maria blamed herself. Maria said she was going through penance. Maria screamed, cried; Maria, the mother of the Black boys, suffered. Maria, who, like many Black mothers, needed to get up every day and go to work. Maria needed to take care of four children. Maria, who was a mother, provider, friend, accomplice, and emotional support, was now Maria without ground.

The next day, the family from the community went looking for the boy in the dump field. They walked a lot. An older resident said it was so everyone could follow the vulture's tracks. The people who collected things from the landfill also became aware of this and helped. Everyone there was looking for Pedro. Many bodies were found. Many. Lots of Black bodies. Towards the end of the afternoon, a child at the dump said he had seen Pedro. Everyone ran to the place, scaring away the vultures, and there he was, lying down. Very hurt. Very.

A woman helping with the search cried, "Why do this to our boys?" Pedro was taken by the community. He was barely breathing. At the hospital, the boy was taken to the emergency room. The community stayed there—an entire community in support of a Black boy.

Maria and Pedro shared the same room in the hospital. Maria only realized this when, still dizzy, she looked to the side and saw what seemed familiar to her: Pedro's black, flat feet. Maria got off the stretcher. "My son, my son, my son..." She leaned over her son's chest and cried. She felt Pedro's heartbeat and said, "Mommy is here." The boy opened his eyes. Tears flowed from his eyes. "Mommy is here," Maria said. Pedro, with great difficulty, said, "Mamma."

16.

The Occlusive Carceral Tactics of White Womanhood

Erica Ewa-Elechi and Joshua Harris

Introduction

On May 25, 2020, the world witnessed the conduct of a Canadian white woman, Amy Cooper, when she phoned the New York police to make a complaint against Christian Cooper, a Black queer man. Sparking the incident was Amy's misconduct in Central Park. She had her dog off leash despite signs stating otherwise, and Christian requested she follow the rules. As an argument began, Christian started recording it for his safety and Amy demanded he stop recording.

As Christian requested that Amy keep her distance, especially because of COVID-19 distancing restrictions, she continued to approach him and told Christian she would call the police and claim an African American man threatened her and her dog. Amy followed through on this threat, called the police, and justified the call based on a false claim Christian yelled at her. Had it not been for Christian's recording, it is possible his name would be among those counted as dead or those dying in carceral systems.

However, this recording captured what we as Black people know to be true about white womanhood and its active and real threat to Black life and livelihood: it is rooted in anti-Black racist violence and white supremacy.

In *On Property*, Rinaldo Walcott describes this phenomenon of white people, and white women in particular, deputizing themselves to police Black people. These white women "refuse to let Black people live their lives, with all the usual assumptions about blackness and property integral to these interactions" (29).

When we wrote this chapter, we did so with a sense of urgency in the wake of the 2020 Black uprisings, and in response to the alleged commitments of various institutions and disciplines, such as social work and child welfare, to better the living conditions of Black life.

It is not our argument that social work or child welfare are spectacular in this deputization; rather, these are our entry points into the broader issue of what we call the occlusive/carceral tactics of white womanhood, which is made possible in their deputization of policing Black life.

We do this theoretical work not to speak to the hearts of white women and white people in general. Instead, we attempt to prepare Black people for the minefield that is white womanhood when advocating and organizing for Black women, Black families, and Black child welfare survivors in areas such as social work and child welfare. Bringing about substantive individual and systemic changes for Black people requires a studied outthinking of whiteness and not getting lost in responding to the weeds of whiteness' semantics that we often find Black people pinned down by when doing freedom-making work.

We are indebted to the writers, thinkers, and organizers from the Black radical tradition and Black feminist thought for providing the necessary critical vocabulary for this chapter which provides an incomplete narrative of Black life in child welfare. Their work makes possible the naming of child welfare as a carceral site in its ongoing histories of white supremacy, anti-Black racism, and colonialism.

Using these various ways of thinking, this chapter outlines our social, political, and historical understandings of the tactics of white womanhood as occlusive/carceral. We then pull this understanding into a case study of community-based advocacy we provided to a young Black mother in November 2018. For confidentiality purposes, we named her Tia.

Tia is also a child welfare survivor and provided enthusiastic consent to discuss her experiences with Halton Children's Aid Society (HCAS) and the white child protection workers from this agency Tia interacted with. We named these white child protection workers Becky and Susie.

HCAS also had a Black staff member hired for the purposes of equity, diversity, and inclusion present, and we named her Britney.

Our chapter contours Becky, Susie, and even Britney's occlusive/carceral tactics they deployed during our advocacy with Tia to illustrate the hold white womanhood attempts to have on Black freedom, and its dangerous and deadly consequences for Black people. We labour to depict these tactics as creating moments of unfreedom embedded in anti-Black racism, misogynoir, respectability politics, and the co-optation of social justice.

We also articulate the kind of radical refusals we made, grounded in our ability to outthink white womanhood's occlusive/carceral tactics. "Our" incorporates Tia's refusals, which included calling upon us as the Black community to be her comrades.

Despite being told it would be impossible to reverse the false verification of neglect by lawyers and the very child protection workers involved in the investigation, our radical refusals grounded in transformative justice and abolition resulted in the supposedly impossible: reversing the false verification of neglect.

Possibility lives beyond the boundaries set by whiteness, anti-Black racism, misogynoir, and their capillaries of neoliberalism and respectability. We want Black readers to understand questioning the "impossible" as a radical and ethical praxis especially when it comes to Black mothers, Black families, and Black child welfare survivors.

Child Welfare Carcerality

We find it necessary to state that child welfare is a carceral system. We are not arguing that child welfare is the same as the criminal justice system. However, we place child welfare in the ever-growing carcerality Black people experience across many systems. This carcerality flows directly from a history of Black people's captivity and surveillance during the Transatlantic Slave trade period.

Christina Sharpe argues that we must see our present lives as constantly living in the wake of the operating logics, laws, and institutions that made Black people's enslavement possible (15). Therefore, when it comes to child welfare, we as Black people are constantly coming up against this ongoing history of dehumanization, dispossession, containment, and harmful/deathly practices that live on in this so-called caring system we call child welfare.

Since the first slave ship which forcibly brought enslaved African peoples to other lands such as Canada, white supremacist and anti-Black constructions denied and refused notions of Black family, parenthood, and childhood (Sharpe). This denial included fracturing Black families as an expression of white supremacist power, in which slave traders and owners would steal and sell Black babies and children from Black mothers to other slave owners (Browne 42). These forced movements were displays of power to illustrate enslavers' control over the life and death of Black people generally, as well as for the enslaver's financial benefit. (Browne).

The general denial of Black personhood, including for Black women and children, justified and allowed for abhorrent but daily forms of deathly and death-making violence towards Black people, who were considered property (Sharpe 21).

In "The Meaning of Motherhood in Black Culture and Mother-Daughter Relationships," Patricia Hill Collins described how Black mothers resisted this power by caring for their own and others' children, even from long distances, and would go as far as fighting for freedom by running from the plantation with their children (4-6).

This history of managing Black families through the denial of Black family life continued after slavery's abolition in the form of anti-Black state policies and practices that reconstituted this denial and fracturing and sought to relegate and maintain Black people's economic and social marginalization (Collins, *Black Feminist Thought* 58–75). Excluding Black people from state and civil participation relegated Black people to low-income occupations (Roberts 25–33).

Ironically, while Black women and mothers were deemed unfit to be considered mothers, one of the only forms of employment for Black women was, contradictorily, working in the homes of white people and raising white children (Collins, *Black Feminist Thought* 62–65).

During the development of laws regarding families, such as child welfare, white women were increasingly deputized and given legitimate authority over Black mothers' and women's lives and the ability to police Black families (Roberts 7-10). Child and family-related laws became one vehicle for white women to express and enacted misogynoiristic violence against Black women.

Misogynoir refers to the systemic and societal antagonism, denigration, harm and violence directed at Black women (Trudy). The presence of misogynoir in the child welfare system is well documented, for example in how Black mothers come to be mistreated through unethical, anti-Black, assuming, and blaming investigations (Roberts 1–6) and through rigid, classist, unsupportive, and unrealistic reunification plans (OACAS 65–69).

The justification for primarily white women's interactions with Black mothers and families is mostly done through alleged concerns of neglect, which is a direct result of the systemically enforced economic poverty of Black communities (OACAS 22).

These investigations participate in a long history of marking and branding Black people, whereby the investigation follows the family forever (Lamers, "From Topic"). When a parent is put under investigation, or a child is involved in child welfare, that status is passed down to their children (Lamers, "From Topic"). Should an investigation happen for a child, the family history of child welfare interactions is considered a risk factor and therefore facilitates overrepresentation (Lamers, "From Topic").

Consistent overrepresentation of Black children and youth in child welfare is the result of the system's carcerality (OHRC). We cannot understand this overrepresentation as accidental. From the view of history, white people economically benefit from the dispossession and containment of Black people in child welfare (Lamers, "From Topic"). In the context of child welfare, deputized white women social workers gain income from Black children and youth who are continuously held as property in child welfare. These white women surveil and police Black mothers and families to ensure a steady income.

The carcerality of child welfare is particularly apparent in the experiences of Black child welfare survivors. Black child welfare survivors experience overt and covert anti-Black racism through being called "thugs," "sluts," and racial slurs as well as blatant differential mistreatment and an overreliance on police and discipline as parenting (Lamers, "From Topic"; OACAS 39–40).

The multiple placements and forced movement of Black children into white households through various legal processes signify the ongoing history of shipping Black children away from Black families and communities (Lamers, "From Topic"). Meanwhile, child welfare survivors in general statistically graduate high school at 44 per cent, and Black child welfare survivors are likely to be shipped into other carceral systems, such as youth/adult criminal justice or psychiatric systems, or experience homelessness (OACAS 37).

Black child welfare survivors experience being refused support because of their sexuality and gender identity, particularly queer and trans people (Lamers, "From Topic"). This specific reality for Black child welfare survivors comes in tandem with the generally reported experiences of physical, sexual, emotional, mental, and spiritual abuse consistently reported in child welfare (Lamers, "From Topic").

Ultimately, child welfare contains and manages the bodily, spiritual, mental, and physical autonomy of Black child welfare survivors. Should we resist deputized white women social workers and foster home guardians, we are funneled into further carcerality, such as the criminal punishment, psychiatric, and state welfare systems which heavily surveil those in need.

Theorizing the Occlusive and Carceral Tactics of White Womanhood

White supremacist constructions of gender include historical constructions of white womanhood developed in response to Blackness as one way to contain Black people. Black feminist thinkers and scholars, such as bell hooks, Patricia Hill Collins, Trudy, and Moya Bailey, help name the kinds of dangerous and deathly antagonisms white womanhood presents towards Black people.

Patriarchal constructs of white womanhood presented true femininity as piety, purity, submissiveness, and domesticity—something only white women during slavery could live up to given that Black women were not even considered to be in the category of human and therefore woman (Collins, *Black Feminist Thought* 53–54). Black women's embodiment was already inherently excluded from this white gender construction of femininity. Therefore, Black women's subjugation to extreme forms of labour and abhorrent violence was justified.

However, under slavery, white women were not just passive observers of the subjugation and dehumanization of Black women and people; instead, they played an active role in this process. White women's historical position of working in the home meant they actively surveilled Black people, often Black women, working inside their homes (Collins, *Black Feminist Thought* 62–63). White women were even capable of owning

Black people as slaves in a period where white women were also considered property, albeit very differently than Black people (Walcott 22).

This deputization of white women accompanied what Collins describes as the controlling images of Black women. One controlling image of Black women is the "Mammy" meaning the good subservient obedient Black woman house worker willing to sacrifice her own life and family for the wellbeing of the white family (Collins, *Black Feminist Thought* 79). Other images portray Black women as aggressive and out of control if they do not conform to the controlling image (83–92). Therefore, through these controlling images, white women could legitimately police and surveil Black women.

Historical laws criminalizing Black men as rapists for engaging in sexual relations with white women meant Black masculinity was constructed as an inherent threat to white womanhood (57). Between Black femininity being constructed as aggressive if not obedient and Black masculinity as inherently terrifying and dangerous, is white women's ability to assert their deputized white supremacist power through acting and embodying being terrified and harmed. After supposed emancipation, white women from benevolent societies adopted a white saviour role by going to the American South to teach supposedly emancipated Black people (du Bois 20).

Yet, if white women narrated history, they relegate themselves to merely the oppressed individual who had no power in relation to her white husband. This is the first broad function of white womanhood: It occludes the deputized role given to white women socially and in fields like social work and child welfare.

By occlude, we mean white womanhood inherently misdirects accountability away from the person engaging in violence and harm and who holds systemic and terrifying power. Instead, white womanhood points the view back onto the Black person, who is already constructed as terrifying and monstrous through ongoing historical anti-Black constructions.

These occlusions occur through the gendered constructions of whiteness and Blackness mentioned earlier and can include other intersections not described in this chapter. These occlusions maintain white supremacy and anti-Black racism, causing almost immediate pivots away from substantive redress, slowing and halting possible shifts at the systemic, institutional, and individual levels.

In the realm of social work and child welfare, this is dangerous for Black people, especially for Black mothers and child welfare survivors, who are already vulnerable and made precarious by systemic and state surveillance amid anti-Black controlling images. Instead of white women social workers, institutions, and the state being held accountable for this violence, it is the Black precarious client who must apologize because of occlusive misdirections.

Another broad function of white womanhood is carcerality. Woven into the occlusions is the carcerality of containing and controlling Black people in individual situations, especially when Black people's actions do not align with white women's expectations. This carcerality of white womanhood quickly creates unsafe and unliveable spaces and moments of unfreedom for Black people.

White women act as gatekeepers and practitioners of carceral systems, where white women may call the police or surveil Black people in their role of social worker in a way that maintains Black people's carcerality in the system. For example, manufactured lies calling Black people aggressive when we assert ourselves.

Carcerality includes the ability to call human resource departments and engage in certain occlusions that result in Black people's unemployment or being pushed out of institutions, such as academia. White women can even be the subject of a Black person's complaint and still pivot the dynamic to result in the Black complainer's unemployment.

White women know they have this power. The case of Amy Cooper shows she knew she could make a false call to the police and embody white womanhood in a particular manner that could result in Christian Cooper's possible carcerality and death. If not for the recording, Amy's façade of tears in response to Christian holding her accountable may have achieved her goal. An important fact is that Amy Cooper was from Canada when this incident occurred in the United States (US). Clearly, the occlusive and carceral functions of white womanhood do not respond to borders. We should ask what it means for Amy Cooper to be from Canada, a country that sees itself as better than the US. Could it be true that Amy Cooper and her behaviour are only possible because Canada is both occlusive and carceral?

One only needs to look at the many examples of white women calling the police in Canada and the US on Black people literally doing anything: barbequing, swimming in their local pool, picking up garbage on their front lawn, babysitting white children, sleeping in a dormitory common room, playing golf, trying to cash a paycheck, asserting the validity of a coupon, returning from a late night at work, staying at an Airbnb, and removing items from one's own business (Molina). White women have also called the police on Black children selling hot dogs and water and for mowing lawns. These are just the examples we hear about.

Not all these instances were at the hands of white women, such as the Starbucks incident where racialized staff called police on a Black man for sitting too long in the establishment, only later to find out he was a real estate agent waiting for a client (Molina). The culpability and complicity of white cisgender straight men, white LGBT people, Indigenous peoples, and racialized people with the tactics of white womanhood occur through these communities' own use of anti-Blackness. This includes Black people engaging in respectability politics, which acquiesce to, and sometimes support, the occlusive and carceral functions of white womanhood. White supremacy and anti-Black racism allow for anti-Black anxieties and antagonisms, which many people, not just white women, deploy against Black people.

The predictable carcerality of white womanhood results in emotional, mental, physical, and spiritual exhaustion for Black people who navigate white womanhood. We must always be on alert to experience, navigate, and survive these tactics and their possible implications.

These historical, social, and political understandings provide critical entry points in naming and contouring the tactics of white womanhood used to maintain white supremacy and anti-Blackness. We describe these specific tactics as 1) tactics of forgetting; 2) treating Blackness as threatening; and 3) removing individual accountability from workers and avoiding possible redress to harmed Black people—in this case Tia.

At stake is Black people's lives, and in this specific instance, Tia was at risk of losing her daughter due to accusations that came from the day care which resulted in HCAS' investigation. Contouring these tactics allows Black people to outthink the occlusive and carceral functions of white womanhood while also seeing just how carceral child welfare is for Black mothers, Black families, and Black child welfare survivors.

Case Study: Tia and Halton CAS (HCAS)

In November of 2018, we were approached by a Black community member who described Tia's experience and asked if we could attend an upcoming meeting with Tia at HCAS. The year prior, a daycare staffed by all white people reported Tia to HCAS for neglectful behaviour.

Before being reported, Tia raised concerns about the daycare staff's treatment of her child. This went ignored, but shortly afterward Tia learned the daycare staff falsely claimed Tia drove her toddler to the daycare without a car seat. Shortly after this claim, the daycare reported Tia to HCAS for neglect, falsely claiming Tia did not provide her child with the proper resources: shoes.

In their report, the daycare staff claimed Tia never provided diapers, yet Tia repeatedly caught the daycare staff using the diapers that Tia provided for her child, for other children and told them to stop. The daycare also reported the false claim about the car seat and mentioned, for no apparent reason, that Tia had purchased a new vehicle. However, the daycare staff knew Tia's old vehicle broke down. The final "event" which resulted in the daycare's call to HCAS was the daycare's false claim that Tia sent her toddler to daycare with unsafe shoes and that Tia was easily offended and hostile towards offered help.

The daycare informed Tia of the report to HCAS when she arrived at the daycare to pick up her child and her toddler had no shoes on. When Tia asked where the shoes were, the daycare said a child protection worker confiscated them and when Tia asked why HCAS interacted with her toddler, the daycare worker said they could not say anything further, since HCAS would investigate.

When the investigation began, Tia pulled her toddler from the daycare and the daycare then went out of their way—for no reason and no legal grounds—to contact Halton Subsidy to have them deny Tia subsidies. Halton Subsidy provides subsidies to low-income parents for resources such as day care. The daycare claimed Tia was aggressive, yelled at daycare staff, and harassed them over the phone.

This was all untrue. During the reported alleged incident, Tia merely dropped her toddler off and explained to the daycare worker the child did not have shoes because Tia's mother did not have them, but Tia planned to return with a pair. The daycare worker at that time said Tia did not need to go home and return with shoes because the daycare could use a spare pair.

When Tia picked up her toddler, she returned the borrowed shoes to the daycare worker and thanked them. It was afterward, upon learning of the daycare's report to HCAS, when Tia requested to have a meeting with the daycare staff member present the day of the shoes being borrowed because she wanted the daycare employee to be honest about what happened. The daycare worker claimed she could not remember what happened, and Tia reasonably challenged the narrative.

After this, Tia decided to disenroll her child from the day care, and Tia called the daycare once and her mother twice to collect the toddler's belongings, but nobody answered. Tia even recorded the brief conversation over the phone to ensure the daycare could not claim that she was aggressive or threatening. The daycare later claimed this was Tia harassing the daycare.

The lead investigator from HCAS, a white woman, whom we name Becky, investigated the daycare's many claims against Tia and her mothering. When Becky attended Tia's home to investigate, Becky said everything was great and found the daycare's claims about the car seat unfounded. When Becky spoke to Tia's doctor, the doctor said that Tia's toddler was well taken care of, but there were issues around slow development related to the toddler's premature birth.

During the home investigation, Becky asked Tia to give Becky the shoes that were a part of the daycare's report to HCAS. Tia was shocked and told Becky the daycare said Becky confiscated the shoes. Becky said this was impossible because HCAS does not have that kind of legal authority.

As the investigation reached its final stages, Tia was still waiting for her toddler's belongings from the daycare, so Becky agreed to get them. When Becky finally dropped off the bin the daycare packed for Tia, Tia saw the missing shoes sitting at the very top of the bin. Tia showed Becky the shoes and told her that the shoes' condition was not what they looked like when her toddler was last wearing them two weeks prior. Specifically, the shoes had black drag marks and were worn out, as if they had been dragged on a black surface. Becky said everything was okay. She knew Tia was a good mother.

To Tia's shock, a few weeks later, she received a letter from HCAS; they disconfirmed poor parenting but verified neglect. The letter provided no reasoning for their decision. At the time, Tia attempted to address this neglect claim but was told she had to engage in a different process.

But she received no response. Considering all the narrative violence, Tia chose to take some time to heal from the emotional and psychological impact the investigation and reporting had on her.

In the summer of 2018, Tia again attempted to uncover the reasons why HCAS verified neglect in her case. She received a response from Becky's white woman supervisor, whom we call Susie. Susie told Tia she would get back in touch, and over a month later, in September 2018, Tia received no response and emailed requesting an answer. Susie responded in early October of 2018, and said HCAS verified neglect solely because of the contentious shoes, which according to HCAS were too small and were affecting the toddler's development.

Upon receiving this information, Tia requested a meeting with Susie and Becky and connected with us to join the meeting. Using this one hour and thirty-minute meeting, we seek to highlight the occlusive and carceral tactics of white womanhood and the kinds of responses we deployed to disrupt the efficacy of these tactics.

The First Occlusive and Carceral Tactic: Deployment of Forgetting

Lisa Lowe described what she called the ontology of forgetting, as how an individual can "not know" something or someone or "not know" to do something, as well as the active forgetting of important information, realities, and histories. This lack of knowing and active forgetting is lodged within one's subjectivities within power relations of race, gender, sexuality, disability, class, geography, citizenship status, etc. What ends up being forgotten is often that which could aid in intervening against violent logics, conduct, procedures, and policies.

For us, a particular tactic of white womanhood is we call *the deployment of forgetting*, whereby white women claim to not know or forget pertinent information. Its distracting and destructive function forces Black people to educate others at our personal expense while navigating politics of believability, tone policing, and requests to be patient with others' supposed journeys to anti-oppression.

If we tell white women to do their own work, such as reading and researching, this tactic further demonizes us for supposedly being uncompromising, uncooperative, rude, nasty, and unfair.

Becky, Susie, and Britney utilized this tactic in a variety of ways when we met with them. The first thing we chose to address with Becky, Susie, and Britney was the antagonistic behaviour of the daycare staff towards Tia. This included Becky's admission that the report contained false accusations and that the "missing" shoes were in the daycare's possession.

We asked Becky to explain how her investigation solely focused on Tia, and not the conduct of the daycare, after Becky came to learn of the daycare's actions towards Tia. We asked Becky why the information she knew did not help Becky question the good faith of the report or think through the presence of anti-Black racism. Becky claimed that those aspects, at least separately, did not strike her as antagonistic or reason enough to question the report's good faith or think about anti-Black racism.

Causing the most alarm was Becky's inability to critically think about the shoes that had gone missing based on the daycare's claim that they were confiscated by HCAS. In the meeting, we questioned how these shoes could hold so much weight in the investigation and be the sole justification that substantiated and verified neglect.

We asked Becky and Susie explain how it was they gave so much weight to the compromised "evidence", and both responded with "We didn't think about it" and "I don't know." Becky claimed she was so worried about the impact of the shoes on the child's development, that this was her focus.

Here, we see how the state imbued white women social workers in child welfare with a level of power that is more unquestioned than that of the criminal justice system and police. A piece of evidence can go missing for two weeks, be found in the possession of the very people who made the initial report on a low-income single Black mother and child welfare survivor and then be considered viable to justify neglect.

Becky's deployment of forgetting is not only occlusive in our conversation. Her occlusion allowed the shoes to perform a specific function for her view of the investigation and nothing else.

Tia also challenged Becky and explained that her child's shoe size may seem inappropriate for her age only if people did not know that her toddler had been born prematurely. Becky said that she was not aware of this, but Tia reminded her about the time she told Becky about her toddler's premature birth. "Well, I guess I forgot," said Becky.

Tia was being constructed as an irresponsible mother for not conveying all the information to Becky, even though she had. Becky's inability to hear, listen, and understand what Tia told her was directly connected with forgetting. It is easy to forget something you do not want—or care—to hear. To disrupt this, we highlighted the doctor's report that explicitly mentioned development and asked Becky why this item did not register with her if her concern was development. "I don't know," Becky said.

Another way Becky and Susie deployed forgetting was through their assertion they did not consider the daycare workers' or Tia's race, and a complete lack of understanding their own relations to power as white women investigating a Black low-income single mother's experience with the daycare.

This forgetting could possibly be explained, but not justified, by the fact that Becky and Susie are two white women and therefore lack the consciousness required to think about and deal with anti-Black racism in an ethical manner.

However, both Becky and Susie were supposed to know better. HCAS falls under the Child, Youth, and Families Services Act (2017), which attempts to address the overrepresentation of Black children and youth in care. Its preamble describes the need for overrepresentation to be addressed through a race-conscious practice by child protection workers. The change in law required both Becky and Susie to be trained on these changes, which they were.

Moreover, Becky and Susie should have known better because both told us they read a report by the One Vision One Voice Project, a project embedded within the Ontario Association of Children's Aid Societies. This project and its report specifically interrogated and put forward recommendations to address the anti-Black racism within Ontario's child welfare system, especially overrepresentation (OACAS).

Becky and Susie read the report and attended trainings which should have led to some meager display of critical consciousness. When asked why they did not ground themselves in this knowledge, they either said, "I don't know" or "We're still learning."

For Becky and Susie to forget during the investigation means that they do not consider Black life, experiences, knowledge and acts of resistance as valid. Therefore, during a critical moment—that is, investigating a low-income single Black mother—their forgetting allows for them to invade Tia's life and make false and unethical claims that have life-long and dangerous implications for Tia and her child.

The Second Occlusive and Carceral Tactic: The Threat of Blackness

The insidious and readily available tactic of constructing *Blackness as a threat* is a powerful tool in the deputization of white women in social work. It is this tactic that we find anti-Black anxieties and antagonisms to be the most obvious.

The tactic of the threat of Blackness refers to methods and devices deployed to criminalize, demonize, and pathologize Black expression that resists anti-Blackness and white supremacy; it helps to maintain white supremacy and anti-Black racism (Abdillahi). Idil Abdillahi argues that Blackness, and more specifically Black emotionality, is always constructed as madness and therefore treated with deathly carcerality in various systems.

Black expression in this respect means both the perceptions of and the embodiment of our physical bodies, such as body posture, facial expressions, verbal and written reactions, and emotionality. We could be tall or fat and this will be constructed differently as a threat and used against Black people to justify expressions of fear and violence, often with harmful and deathly results (Mallow 111–12).

The anti-Black respectable logic operating here is that there is some space where the reception of Black resistance happens. Black people just need to learn how to access it by articulating ourselves in a nice and respectable way and trust the supposed goodness of those who violate and oppress us. This tactic is a form of emotional, psychological, and spiritual carcerality because it allows for us to be blamed for not accessing this fictional space within white institutions and organizations (Samudzi and Anderson 64). We are blamed for not using a vocabulary of niceness, politeness, and respectability, which will not bring about Black people's liberation. Instead, this tactic results in collective containment for Black communities and punishment for certain Black individuals (13).

The questioning we used to disrupt forgetting resulted in the deployment of Blackness as a threat, as questioning from Black people was perceived as threatening. When Becky claimed that the shoes were affecting the toddler's development, we asked specific questions about her ability to make such an appraisal.

We asked if Becky had any education or training in understanding the development of babies, toddlers, and children and what could delay it. Becky responded with "no." We asked how Becky came to make this appraisal. She said that when she saw the shoes on the toddler during her initial visit at the daycare before Tia knew HCAS had been activated, she saw red impression marks along the toddler's ankle. We quickly lifted the pants around our ankles to show red marks from our socks and shoes to exemplify how this was not sufficient to confirm her appraisal.

We asked if she sought medical advice to confirm this was affecting the toddler's development. Becky said, "No."

Then, Becky turned red with tears in her eyes and said, "Why do I feel like I'm on the stand?! Who are you people?"

The tears and redness signal that we are a threat in our questioning. To disrupt this, we reminded her of our professional background as social workers. We told her we hoped she would consider asking these questions as an aspect of the critical social work she espoused.

Our refusal to acquiesce could have had carceral consequences: police, arrest, or containment. It could have maintained Tia's carcerality in child welfare. Becky's comparison of our questioning to that of being interrogated occluded the unequal power dynamic that existed in the space. Our questioning did not have the same institutional or systemic power or have the same implications as theirs did. Becky and Susie's questioning of Tia's life had the potential to mark her for life and undo her entire family.

Closely connected to Black people's questioning being considered a threat is Black people's direct critical analyses manufactured as a threat. When we analyzed the situation, Becky and Susie saw it as distracting. The two consistently attempted to fabricate a goal of moving forward and presented our critical analyses as getting in the way of that goal. We challenged this tactic by stating that our goal was to reverse the verification of neglect. We stated as Black people concerned with collective freedom, we also wanted everyone to think through how Becky and Susie arrived at the verification in the first place.

Black resistance does threaten Becky and Susie because it threatens the deputized power and innocence they hold and try to maintain. Black people are not powerless in such situations, despite what they may expect. Our ability to strategize, navigate, resist, and refuse reflects the broader implications of Black people's resistance to the current social order and racial hierarchies, providing pathways to new possibilities. The ability to continuously expose their anti-Black conduct is dangerous for the status quo; it threatens white women's ability to engage in anti-Black racism unencumbered.

The Third Occlusive and Carceral: The Removal of Accountability and Redress

Becky and Susie tended to point the finger at someone or something else to avoid accountability or responding to Tia's demands for redress. This blatant scapegoating used to *avoid accountability and redress* is the third tactic we describe. Becky's and Susie's occlusive "point and run" method was meant to shut down questioning or have us just end the discussion. It performed a carceral function by trying to have us either become further embattled with the child welfare system, the daycare, or be embattled with their Black colleague HCAS who attended the meeting with Becky and Susie.

The removal of accountability occurred in relation to the verification of neglect, as Becky and Susie stated they could not reverse it. The online system did not make this possible. Only the online system is to be blamed.

In response to our continuous naming of the daycare's report as anti-Black, Becky and Susie used their Black colleague, Britney, as what we call their Black line of defence. This refers to the widely discussed reflex of white/non-Black people pointing to the Black people they know, or know of, to avoid addressing their anti-Black racism.

Susie explained that part of the reason why the verification of neglect occurred was because Britney was away on leave at the time of the investigation. Britney's absence, according to Susie, meant she and Becky had nobody to consult with and help them think through their investigation.

This was an attempt by Susie to make Britney completely accountable for all HCAS' actions and to conscript Britney into being Susie and Becky's moral and ethical compass when it comes to addressing anti-Black racism. By this logic only Britney is "really" accountable to Black people, not Becky and Susie.

When called upon, Britney reiterated Susie's excuse and then described all the supposed good things HCAS was doing to address anti-Black racism. Britney also told us that upon a reflection meeting that had occurred the day before our meeting, Becky and Susie understood how problematic the daycare's report was. It is in these responses from Britney where she became HCAS' Black line of defence.

Important here is that a Black person's presence does not necessarily mean substantive change. The misplaced applause for diversity, equity, inclusion, and anti-oppression, or their representation, occludes the ongoing anti-Black climate in these institutions. For us, and Tia, to experience what we did exposes how representation does not mean liberation; instead, Britney is employed to do the institution's work.

To act alongside Becky and Susie in the way she did illustrates one of our main points: Black people can be complicit in the same kind of undignified harms that Becky and Susie enacted. We are not suggesting that Black people not be hired in positions, but rather we need to be honest that the role of certain Black people in violent institutions like child welfare is to be the cooperative diversity mule acting against Black freedom.

The reality is that most institutions do not want Black freedom. As Black feminist activist, organizer, and cofounder of the Black Action Defence Committee Angela Robertson says, Black people, like Britney, inside these institutions need to consider their own personal ethics. Robertson advised Black people on the inside need to act as informants for Black communities—rather than be informants for these institutions.

Conclusion: Practising the Impossible

We understand that our naming of whiteness in the occlusive and carceral tactics of white womanhood is not new. However, we felt it necessary to name the conditions existing for Black mothers, Black families, and Black child welfare survivors under the deputization of white women and those nonwhite individuals willing to acquiesce and support these tactics in child welfare organizations and more broadly.

We made the impossible happen, however, by engaging in radical refusals at every turn of occlusion. In April 2019, we were officially informed that HCAS contacted the IT department and officially reversed the verification of neglect that could have marked Tia and her family for generations. Our relentless questioning and centering of Black people won. To borrow from Sharpe, our intervention brought "breath" to Black people in this moment (109) and provides a particular kind of opening for Black people dealing with child welfare organizations.

But we do not want Tia's experience, our work, and the conduct of HCAS and the daycare to be considered spectacular. Throughout many facets of Black life, the deputization of white womanhood fosters consistent anti-Black attitudes. We must understand that Tia's story was made possible by a long history of white supremacy and anti-Blackness in the social work profession.

Many of those we had to call peers in our undergraduate and graduate degrees in social work will happily step into this deputized role, which social work has legitimized. Our former instructors—whether white, racialized, Black, or Indigenous—showed themselves to be actively on duty to dehumanize Black social work students (Lamers, "In the Hold"). We know that people such as Becky, Susie, and Britney are socially produced by this white supremacist and anti-Black climate.

For Black people, thirty-minute meetings turn into two-hour lectures, and three-hour lectures can last a lifetime. Walks between classes, conversations in the lunchroom, and even drinks in mixed company morph into marches through history and for our very lives. These meetings, lectures, and experiences are not just figuratively long. They are long because of the physical, mental, emotional, and spiritual exhaustion imposed on us through dynamics of power such as the tactics of white womanhood we described here. But, through knowledge given by our ancestors and teachings handed down from Black educators, writers, scholars, theorists, parents, siblings, lovers, and friends, the occlusive and carceral can be made discernable.

Works Cited

Browne, Simone. *Dark Matters: On the Surveillance of Blackness*. Duke University Press, 2015.

Child, Youth and Family Services Act, 2017. Pub. L. SO 2017, c. 14, Sched. 1. 20 November 2020. https://www.ontario.ca/laws/statute/17c14. Accessed 1 Mar. 2021.

Collins, Patricia Hill. "The Meaning of Motherhood in Black Culture and Black Mother/Daughter Relationships." *SAGE*, vol. 4, no. 2, 1997, pp. 3–10.

Collins, Patricia Hill. *Black Feminist Thought*. Routledge, 2000.

Du Bois, W.E.B. *The Souls of Black Folk*. Dover, 1994.

Lamers, Josh. "In the Hold of the Ship: Surviving the Unrelenting Anti-Black Racism at Ryerson's School of Social Work." *Medium*, 17 Oct. 2019, https://josh-lamers94.medium.com/in-the-hold-of-the-ship-surviving-the-unrelenting-anti-black-racism-at-ryersons-school-of-social-fb797c1f3aaf. Accessed 1 Mar. 2021.

Lamers, Josh, "From Topic and Evidence to Architect: The Development of Black Diasporic Interpretative Phenomenology and the Resistive Strategies of Black Child Welfare Survivors." *The Myth of Child Protection: An Equity Guide to Change*. Edited by Rona Julla van Ouden Hoven, et al. Garant, 2022, pp. 45–74.

Lowe, Lisa. *Immigrant Acts: On Asian American Cultural Politics*. Duke University Press, 1996.

Mallow, Anna. "Unvictimizable: Toward a Fat Black Disability Studies." *African American Review*, vol. 50, no. 2, 2017, pp. 105–21.

Molina, Brett. "Cashing Checks, Napping, More Activities Leading to Police Calls on Black People in 2018." *USA Today*, 20 Dec. 2018, https://www.usatoday.com/story/news/nation/2018/12/20/black-people-doing-normal-things-who-had-police-called-them-2018/2374750002/. Accessed 27 Dec. 2024.

Monsebraaten, Laurie. "Toronto Children's Aid Worker Launches Human Rights Case Claiming On-the-Job Racism." *The Toronto Star*, 20 Nov. 2018, https://www.theguardian.com/world/2024/dec/27/azerbaijan-airlines-plane-experienced-external-interference-before-crash. Accessed 27 Dec. 2024.

Ontario Association of Children's Aid Society (OACAS). "One Vision One Voice: Changing the Ontario Child Welfare System to Better Serve African Canadians—Practice Framework Part 1: Research Report." *OACAS*, 2016, https://www.oacas.org/wp-content/uploads/2016/09/One-Vision-One-Voice-Part-1_digital_english-May-2019.pdf. Accessed 27 Dec. 2024.

Ontario Human Rights Commission (OHRC). "Interrupted Childhoods: Over-representation of Indigenous and Black Children in Ontario Child Welfare." *OHRC*, 2018, https://www3.ohrc.on.ca/en/interrupted-childhoods-over-representation-indigenous-and-black-children-ontario-child-welfare. Accessed 27 Dec. 2024.

Roberts, Dorothy. *Shattered Bonds: The Color of Child Welfare*. Basic Civitas Books, 2002.

Roberston, Angela. "Everyday Activism, Critical Resistance: A Conversation with Angela Robertson and Robyn Maynard Facilitated by Dionne Brand." York University, Toronto, 15 Feb. 2018. Public Lecture.

Samudzi, Zoe, and William C. Anderson. *As Black as Resistance: Finding the Conditions for Black Liberation.* AK Press, 2018.

Sharpe, Christina. *In the Wake: On Blackness and Being.* Duke University Press, 2016.

Trudy. "Explanation of Misogynoir." *Gradient Lair,* 28 Apr. 2014.

Walcott, Rinaldo. *On Property.* Biblioasis, 2021.

17.

"I Beat Yo' Ass": Spanking in Multigenerational Immigrant Families

Christina Santi

I found out I was pregnant on August 5, 2017. At first, I was excited to create a family with my partner, even if it came as a surprise. Things were different, and I would be the first woman in my family not to be a teenage mom. One week later, the Unite the Right rally took place in Charlottesville, Virginia. It was one of the most violent public assemblies by neo-Nazis and far-right extremists in decades. Before I felt my unborn child's first kick, I was worried about them being born during a white supremacist movement. I wondered why I wanted to bring another Black child into the world.

"Chrissy will be a free-range parent," my cousin Simone said in the family WhatsApp chat after finding out I was expecting. I imagined my brood of aunts collectively sighing, knowing another conversation about childhood trauma was brewing. "You all had a good life. We did all we could with what we had. This talk of trauma because you *got your ass beat* here and there is nonsense," my aunt BJ said, cutting the conversation off before it got legs.

She was coyly referencing the discussion we had after I shared the lyrics to "FEAR.," a song by Kendrick Lamar off his Pulitzer-prize-winning album *DAMN*. In the first verse track, the then twenty-nine-year-old rapper explores the fears and worries he had at seven years old. At the forefront of his terror was having an austere mother while also navigating the equally terrifying danger of the hood. Kendrick uses the anaphora "I beat yo' ass" to depict how his mother used or threatened violence as a fear tactic.

> I beat yo' ass, you keep talkin' back
> I beat yo' ass, who bought you that?
> You stole it, I beat yo' ass if you say that game is broken
> I beat yo' ass, you jump on my couch

Although it was a familiar fear, hearing the song was my first realization that the use of violence mirrored what my Black parents experienced from the world at large.

"Yo! Come outside."

Hearing my best friend, LaKeisha, shout under my window was always the start of a mischievous summer day in the Bronx. We would all gather to hang out on someone's stoop, ride our bikes for miles, and share cold-cut sandwiches and twenty-five-cent juices from the bodega. We dared to live mimicking the adults in our lives, eager to feel this perceived freedom every day.

One afternoon, I was sitting on a curb enjoying a pack of Round Up bubble gum cigarettes I bought off the ice cream truck. In the distance, Timothy, my cousin, with whom I was inseparable, failed to land any of the three pointers he threw into a grimy trash can. Lakiesha and her legion of cousins came over and asked us to play. Ordinarily, I would have been up for whatever scheme they proposed, but they came carrying a BB gun to shoot pigeons in the park. If there was one thing my aunts always told us, it was to never under any circumstance play with guns. Even gun finger gestures were off-limits. I often think about how such a strict rule could have saved twelve-year-old Tamir Rice's life that afternoon on a Cleveland playground in November 2014.

My cousin was intrigued by the taste of coolness that came with the innocent violence of taking out a helpless bird. He grabbed the weapon, brandishing it as if he was the most powerful man in the world. Not two seconds later, my aunt BJ appeared on the block, returning early from her double shift as an operating room nurse. The shock and rage on her face seemed to meet us at eye level even though she stood over a foot above our nine-year-old frames.

Immediately, the crowd of children dispersed, knowing the scenario would end with a spanking. Each of us in the group had witnessed the other get beaten in some capacity for disobedience. My aunt commanded both my cousin and me into the apartment. She yelled like a banshee, waking up her younger sister, who was asleep before a graveyard shift—and signalled her daughter, my teenage cousin, to hang up on her latest crush. My aunt calling on an audience while physically punishing us added an extra element of discipline: public humiliation.

"How many times do I have to tell you guys the same thing?" She roared before slipping into the Jamaican accent she hid from her coworkers. Aunt BJ swiftly set down her bags, reached for Timothy, and placed him across her lap. She began to give him a mighty whooping. I stood near the dining room table, crying from all the chaos because I knew I would receive a few licks for being an accomplice to his offense. It was typical that if one of us got a beating, we all did. It was our guardians' way of trying to deter future attempts to defy authority.

"Who cyaan 'ear muss feel (who can't hear must feel)," she said after implementing the spanking. This is a play on the "ears to hear, let him hear" phrase, which appears throughout the Gospels and Revelation in the Bible. It is a call to action for people to heed the Word of God. "I do this because I love you," she declared later that evening. "Hitting you hurts me more than it does you."

Most enslaved Africans taken to the United States were not Christians; 20 per cent of the approximately 600,000 Africans were Muslim (PBS). The vast majority of others practiced traditional African religions, which were animistic (Pluralism Project). Many slave parents embraced the monotheistic religion out of force, but some did so to maintain hope and dignity. There was still a great deal of pressure to keep children to become obedient workers who could behave to escape potential torture or separation from their families. My aunt and other Black mothers past and present used the fear described in the Bible to guide children into growing up to be well-behaved. It is a form of discipline that ties us together across the diaspora and mirrors God's teaching, as Kendrick alludes to in the song.

As a first-generation Black American, I share stories with my African American friends about times we were sent to get switches or belts for punishment. We exchange tales of marks from open-handed slaps and being hit with any household items within arm's reach: hangers, shoes, extension cords, and wooden spoons. It did not matter who you were—a mother, an older relative, or a close family friend. Hitting us was permitted as a means to keep us in line. It was a hushed realization that even young Black children should help protect themselves from the potential racially charged consequences of being disobedient in society.

Black parents have legitimate fears about their children's safety, from succumbing to street culture to racialized violence from police. Many, like my community of mothers, believe that physical discipline keeps us on track. However, corporal punishment did not stop them from becoming victims in one way or another of what they feared would harm us. The violence was a product of Bible teachings; it protected us from the streets' dangerous temptations, which could lead to violence, drugs, crime, and early pregnancy. However, my eldest uncle spent more than half his life behind bars before being deported.

My mother gave birth to me at sixteen years old. Teenage pregnancy was a pattern in our family; my grandmother had her first child at seventeen, and all her children became parents before finishing high school. It is how my cousins and I ended up living with my aunt, who was the most capable of raising children among her siblings. Most of the physical punishments we received came from her unresolved traumas—her frustrations of giving up her dreams for her younger sisters and their children.

As an adult, I have come to believe that these spankings were abusive. My younger self deserved someone who would tell her that she mattered and to know someone saw her good qualities more than the times she behaved questionably. Communication could have saved me from the avoidable pain of the world. Instead, forms of abuse followed up with affection became ingrained as forms of love and created what scholar Patrick Carnes coined as trauma bonding: "a strong emotional attachment between an abused person and his or her abuser, formed as a result of the cycle of violence" (qtd. in Austin et al. 67). Experiencing physical violence at home led me to accept that mental and psychological abuse was present in a toxic work environment, other relationships, and earlier acceptance of excessive force by police. I vowed never to lift a finger to hit my future children to avoid trapping them in these unhealthy lopsided relationships.

My aunts and uncles shared tales of growing up in Jamaica with me as a child. When we dared to become too American by claiming agency as children, they would express how hard life was back home. Culturally, children were to do as they were told and to be seen not heard. On different occasions, each of my elders recounted times teachers swapped them with rulers or that distant relatives used violence to put them in line. There was no shortage of disciplinarians once my grandparents left their children on the small island to pursue the American dream. My eldest cousin often speaks of the time she fell out of a mango tree and dislocated her arm after being warned not to climb it. In fear of the consequences, she sat through dinner tolerating the pain by using her other arm to eat. Once our great-grandfather noticed, he delivered hits to the spot before sending her to bed for failing to listen.

Colonialism has had a significant impact on the Black community's use of spankings. The colonization of Jamaica by the British may have influenced the corporal punishment used to discipline children. While there are no direct answers if it is a West African tradition, it cannot be ignored how the pressures of plantation life and Britain's own history of corporal punishment affected West Indian disciplinary actions (Arnold). Famed English writers George Orwell and James Boswell touch upon the link between corporal punishment and classic education in their works. In "Such, Such Were the Joys", an autobiographical essay, Orwell details being spanked at boarding school for bedwetting at eight years old. Boswell's biography *Life of Samuel Johnson*, about the literary genius, chronicles the English writer's upbringing as a sickly child who went to a boarding school where the headmaster "never taught a boy in his life—he whipped and they learned." (Boswell 410). History shows a long link between using force to disciple children in British culture. Research suggests there is no historical evidence that precolonial West African societies disciplined children by physical means (Patton). Instead, children were revered as gods or reincarnated ancestors. During my pregnancy, I began to have vivid memories of my grandmother.

"Your grandmother did not spare the rod at all," my mother revealed to me. "Between her and your grandfather, they had eight kids to keep in line and alive. As the second to last child, getting slapped for having a smart mouth seemed normal. If mommy did not hit me, someone else did." There is a history of the mothers in my family leaving their children to pursue better futures for themselves. When I was a toddler, my mother left to attend Lehigh University. I lived with my maternal grandparents until my grandmother died when I was five years old. Then, I was sent to live with my aunt BJ, the eldest daughter of the Thomas family. Six people lived in the quaint three-bedroom apartment: BJ (her daughter, Simone, who migrated from Jamaica after our granny's funeral), my aunt Angella (and her son Timothy), my aunt Nadine (ten years my senior), and myself.

When my mom would visit, she always asked if I was spanked and would make it known she was against the idea of her daughter being hit. I would never tell her the truth about it. I understood that although she was my mother, actual authority belonged to the women who took care of me each day. "I don't remember ever being antispanking, but I know I didn't spank you as much as I got spanked," my mother said during a conversation about parenting. "I punished you more because I felt that had a bigger impact and was a better deterrent for bad behaviour. Plus, you weren't bad as much as you were quick-lipped. I suppose you get that from me."

I went to live with my mom when I was ten. At twenty-six, she was working full-time, mothering, and attending a graduate program at NYU. Maybe she doesn't remember rejecting spanking because that ideology quickly disappeared once I was under her roof. The whippings were less frequent, but they were just as brutal. I remember being struck with a tennis shoe, waking up to slaps for being forgetful, and being lashed with a belt for not adequately taking care of my little brother or being late coming home from school. For a long time, I would avoid my mother to stay clear of her manic behaviour. I was acutely aware that her tendency to hit me was linked to other issues she did not have the language to communicate.

During sophomore year in high school, I read *All About Love*, the critically acclaimed book by feminist icon bell hooks. In it, hooks writes: "Physically abused children have been taught by parenting adults that love can coexist with abuse. And in extreme cases that abuse is an expression of love. This faulty thinking often shapes our adult perceptions of love" (9). I weighed this against what I observed within my family. Most mothers who openly beat their children had a lack of resources and were often angry at larger systems.

> I beat yo' ass, you know my patience runnin' thin
> I got buku payments to make
> County building's on my ass, tryna take my food stamps away

My mother remembers having to tend to her brother's wounds after NYPD officers brutalized him in the 1980s. My adult relatives back in Jamaica and here in the states have vivid memories of the first time they witnessed or were victims of state-sanctioned violence. When I was five, I saw a cop beat up a young man for hopping a turnstile at a train station. On the same train platform, I would see Black moms pop their children for daring to be too curious. Every time I saw violence used to wield power, I looked away and kept silent. In my young mind, people on the receiving end deserved whatever came to them because it is what happened in my home when any of us did wrong.

Between wanting to survive and be included in the American image, I do not think my community of mothers fully grasped that their attachment to spanking is based on the suffering and violence Black people experience because of colonialism and white supremacy. Historically, the Black body has been controlled through colonialism, slavery, lynching, segregation, sexual violence, policing, and mass incarceration. The more educated I became, the more I agreed with hooks's theories on childhood abuse. My Black parents were reacting to the systemic brutality they experienced every day, whether they were aware of it or not. My mother's mind was open to a worldview, a privilege those of her siblings who raised me never fully understood. "I wish that I hadn't spanked you," she said regretfully. "But when I came home at around 10:00 pm from working two jobs and gearing up to do assignments with two kids, I realize now that I was frustrated often for what happened outside our home and took it out on you."

"With you, I was struggling as a teenager who had to grieve her mother's death." My younger brother was born when I was thirteen (my mom was twenty-nine). He got hit maybe a total of three times in his life. "I was older when I had your brother. My degrees allowed me to have a better job and access to more resources." My mother grew up in a time when children were not believed to experience trauma. I believe this is a side effect of the post-civil-rights era, which Black people endured despite hundreds of years of trauma. Her generation and those before viewed keeping Black children alive as the sole goal of parenting. Access to world viewpoints and other lived experiences outside the confines of urban neighbourhoods allowed her to grow.

Following in her footsteps and being one of the few among my cousins to have a higher education, I also learned how racialized history affects parenting. The cycle of violence is learned and creates continuing generations desensitized to brutality. I am determined to break the generational curse of both being a teen parent and using force as a means of power, often the only power a Black woman can create for herself in society.

> I beat yo' ass if I beat yo' ass twice and you still here
> Seven years old, think you run this house by yourself?
> N***a, you gon' fear me if you don't fear no one else

"FEAR." opens up with a verse from the Old Testament of the Bible, creating a parallel between the fear Kendrick's mom instills in him and that of God's discipline. My family was offended by the power of the metaphor. They would use my academic successes or my financial stability as examples to disprove my point. I was too scared to talk about the violence I endured in a past relationship or the night terrors from brutal spanking. We never spoke about the topic again.

Kendrick's music was a fixture in my life because he gave a voice to the issues Black youth faced growing up in the inner city. He understands my depression, the danger of venturing outside, how parents can be a part of that terror, and the guilt of being the one to make it out. It is why his music became a muse for the Black Lives Matter movement—a social justice movement I flung myself into.

In October 2017, I found out I was having a boy, and an added layer of worry set in. At first, I was outside of Kendrick's narratives because he spoke through the vantage point of being a Black boy and man. The minute I found out I was having a male child that shifted. I thought of Ramarley Graham, the eighteen-year-old shot in the back in his grandmother's apartment by a police officer on February 2, 2012. I envisioned the private home across from the park where I hung out in my teens. I recalled marching past the precinct demanding justice for his life and those of men in my life brutalized by police in the building. The repeated sadness was conjured up for Trayvon Martin later that month and for Mike Brown in 2014. The violence I experienced at home desensitized me to the vile acts against Black bodies. Until college, I did not have the urge to fight against it and considered it just another way of life for people like me.

As my son grew stronger and bigger each day in me, I became more worried about his future existence. As racist ideologies became more overt, I believed my womb would be the safest place he would ever live. I filled journals with pondering thoughts of the moment he would be seen as a thug. Tears plopped on pages knowing I could not protect him. I played Kendrick's music every day of my pregnancy because it was settling the truth. My child was born on April 4, 2018, the fiftieth anniversary of Martin Luther King Jr's assassination and the birth date of Maya Angelou, one of the women who led me to write Black stories. My son's birth was a message directly from God. It had to be. As we sat skin-to-skin just a few hours after a traumatic birth, one in which my white nurse failed to listen to my complaints about an awkward pressure that was a sign of my narrow birthing canal. I feared I would be among the statistics of Black mothers who are three times more likely to die from pregnancy-related causes than their white counterparts (CDC).

I declared at that moment, sitting silently and imagining how quickly my son would go from a cute infant to a perceived and stereotyped violent individual, that I would raise him without inflicting intentional violence on him. We live in a world so entrenched in maintaining the status quo of white supremacist, patriarchal dominance that the choice not to spank him would bring about the radical love hooks always wrote about. To me, a Black woman who quiets herself out of fear of violence at every turn, I hope the absence of violence would allow my son to build a world where he truly knows what it means to experience a liberating love—a love that acts as a mirror for him to be more gentle to everyone, but specifically to the Black girls and women he encounters, and a love that allows him to share his gifts with the world. The fearless kind of love Kendrick muses about in rap form. I hope for him to know a freedom that is not entrenched with racialized and gendered consequences—a freedom that my generation, my mother's generation, and her mother's generation never knew.

Works Cited

Arnold, Elaine. "The Use of Corporal Punishment in Child Rearing in the West Indies." *Child Abuse & Neglect*, vol. 6, no. 2, 1982, pp. 141–45.

Austin, Wendy, et al. *Psychiatric & Mental Health Nursing for Canadian Practice*. Wolters Kluwer/Lippincott Williams & Wilkins, 2010.

Boswell, James, and Rodney Shewan. *The Life of Samuel Johnson*. The Folio Society, 1968.

CDC. "Working Together to Reduce Black Maternal Mortality." *Centers for Disease Control and Prevention*, 9 Apr. 2021, https://www.cdc.gov/healthequity/features/maternal-mortality/index.html. Accessed 27 Dec. 2024.

hooks, bell. *All about Love: New Visions*. Harper Perennial, 2001.

Lamar, Kendrick. "FEAR." *DAMN*. Top Dawg Entertainment, 2017. CD.

Orwell, George. "Such, Such Were the Joys." *The Art of the Personal Essay: An Anthology from the Classical Era to the Present*. Edited by Philip Lopate. Anchor-Doubleday, 1994, pp. 269–302.

Patton, Stacey. "Corporal Punishment in Black Communities: Not an Intrinsic Cultural Tradition but Racial Trauma." *American Psychological Association,* 2017, www.apa.org/pi/families/resources/newsletter/2017/04/racial-trauma. Accessed 27 Dec. 2024.

PBS. "1526-1775: From AFRICA to AMERICA." *This Far by Faith. Journey 1*, Public Broadcasting Service, https://www.pbs.org/thisfarbyfaith/print/journey1.html#:~:text=A%20very%20few%20Africans%20enslaved,which%20were%20animistic%20in%20nature. Accessed 27 Dec. 2024.

Pluralism Project. "Pluralism Project." *The Pluralism Project*, President and Fellows of Harvard College and the Pluralism Project at Harvard University, 18 Mar. 2022, https://pluralism.org/. Accessed 27 Dec. 2024.

18.

fire's rose

Toya Leigh Groves

Have you seen the rose that ^{grew} from Fire
She smokes (inhales) a spliff and never tires (ceaselessly)
She ushers the heat on facades
Breasts on front lines marching (Trampling) safe
beckons rain and washing dishes
rinsing pain and casting wishes
looking from the windowsill
smoked breath sit on top of the hills
hugging onto a little tree
branches cast onto me

                                                           *Suicide Note 6
                                  Have you seen the fires rose
                                        Dancing and twirling
                                                    and
                                                   heating
                                                those Who
                                                shiver in
                                                corners
                                                cold

> Cement written and stories told
> Blazing fires and broken bones
> bombs blast and casted stones
> caught in her twirling skirt
> feet browned tiptoed softly on freedoms dirt

fire rose from mourning sights

death trodden by red and blue-filled nights

fast and feast love

passion tatted in magic glove

and gone into tomorrow

fire rose

warming and never spreading out her sorrow

***(cont) suicide note six**

i love you pain but farewell

tucked into this medicine bag. this aching gut heavy and thicklike. the
        smoke on the walls. of throat
           covering what i cannot say loud
    (held tucked under tongue)

        that was slapped outta mouth

            falling

      to

         a

                      floor

          ressined by

              rape

        roots planted deep in the core of nos. that fell from
scream to whisper. smothered in pillows. painted as blood smears.

on cotton dabbing up
                                  what is left of me.

        —You knew I could take it

            so, you took it

19.

One Day at a Time

Luciane Rocha

The image shows Márcia de Oliveira Silva Jacinto, mother of Henry Gomes de Siqueira, killed at the age of sixteen in a police action in Lins, Rio de Janeiro. Marcia conducted a private investigation to contradict the officers' narrative that Henry was involved with criminality and was shot. She moved the criminal justice system to her favour, and the cops were arrested. For several months after Henry died, Marcia still heard him saying, "Mom, I'm home!" when she entered the house.

20.

Finding Joy in His Joy

Luciane Rocha

The image shows Deize Carvalho, the mother of Andreu Carvalho, jumping in the sunshine. In 2008, Andreu, just seventeen years old, was brutally murdered in Rio de Janeiro, Brazil, by security agents in a juvenile facility the night he was checked in. Deize gathered evidence to contradict the agent's narrative that Andreu tried to escape and fell, hitting his head. Through her activism, she proved that Andreu was tortured and assassinated. Deize, born in the Cantagalo favela, graduated from law school in 2020 and has published two books. Andreu's favourite place was the beach, where Dieze now finds joy.

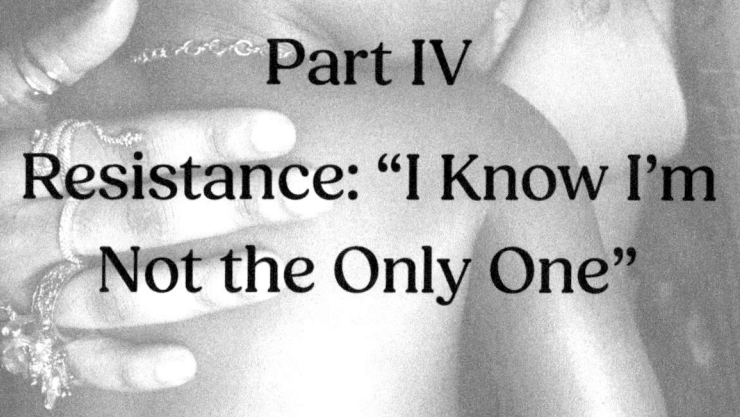

Part IV

Resistance: "I Know I'm Not the Only One"

21.

Protest! Mothering by Example

Luciane Rocha

The picture shows Nésia S. O. Rocha, the mother of author Luciane Rocha, in Pedra do Sal, a Black historical site in downtown Rio de Janeiro. Nesia is a retired seamstress, daughter, and mother of two. She did not have much time to participate in protests when she was younger, working to help her parents take care of six siblings, but she always knew the importance of fighting for what was right. She was young during Brazil's dictatorship and recounts how Black people faced not only physical violence but also symbolic violence; displays of Blackness in aesthetics were a sign of marginality. Nésia is a part of Black cultural activities related to the carnival and supports the annual Black women's march. On her t-shirt is the Duafe, the Adinkra symbol of beauty, and the sticker says: "Pela vida das Mulheres (For Women's Lives)."

22.

"I Am Parenting Black Children for the World": Black Mothers' Insights on State-Sanctioned Violence and the Fight for Black Lives

Seanna Leath, Dawn Demps, and Johari Harris

"Over and over again, we see countless videos, news stories, reports, and statistics about Black children dying, about Black parents suffering, and hear policy after policy being created or used to justify it all" (Story 877). Yet despite the increasing focus on the impact of racial discrimination on Black individuals' health (Mouzon 178), there is less research on how Black mothers' perspectives on racialized violence influence the messages they provide to their children about racial justice and equity. The current chapter focusses on Black mothers' narrative reflections of how they processed viral instances of police brutality in the news amid the resurgent Black Lives Matter protests in 2020. We draw on Black feminist inquiry as a theoretical and methodological lens and individual interview data from thirty-one Black mothers (twenty-five to fifty-two years) across the United States (US). Through thematic analysis, we identified three main themes: (1) limiting social media to reduce vicarious trauma; (2) rejecting respectability politics as a pathway to liberation; and (3) raising the next generation of freedom fighters. The findings highlight the intersection of activism, movement building, and Black mothering in the twenty-first century. We discuss the adaptive messages that Black mothers provided about racial injustice, police brutality, and freedom. This chapter adds to the small but growing body of literature dedicated to providing a sociohistorical understanding of how Black mothers help their children understand racialized violence in American society by integrating their sociopolitical awareness into their parenting practices.

In April 2015, Toya Graham, a Black mother in Baltimore, was filmed slapping and reprimanding her son for participating in the Baltimore protests against police brutality. Graham said she pulled her adolescent son away because "I don't want him to be another Freddie Gray," referring to a twenty-five-year-old Black man who was killed in federal custody. Ms. Graham's words are but one example of the race-related challenges that Black mothers face when raising their children within a society that capitalizes on anti-black racialized violence (Smith 31). There is a need for scholarship that considers how Black parents pass down intergenerational knowledge on interpersonal and institutional racism to their children. This chapter focuses on Black mothers' reflections on how they processed viral instances of police brutality in the news amid the Black Lives Matter protests in 2020.

Given the resurgence of white supremacist visibility in response to Trump's presidency and the countless Black lives lost since Alicia Garza coined the phrase "Black Lives Matter" in 2013, it is important to consider the messages that Black parents provide to their children about racism and state-sanctioned violence. For many Black parents, current events may intensify the belief that effective socialization messages can be the difference between life and death for their children (McClain 5). Furthermore, Black families are exposed to violence against Black people in multiple ways (e.g., personal experiences, television, news outlets, social media, and cell phones); thus, the transmission of intergenerational knowledge and coping skills on racialized violence from Black mothers to their children is an understudied but critical area of research.

Racial Socialization and Black Maternal Activism

Black parents have unique considerations in trying to prepare their children to cope with racial discrimination (i.e., prejudicial treatment of individuals due to their racial group membership) and racially motivated violence in schools, neighbourhoods, and community settings (Cooper

69). Racial socialization, or the messages that parents convey to their children about the meaning of their racial group membership, is a key parenting practice that Black parents use to help their children understand, process, and cope with racial discrimination (Anderson et al. 426). Racial socialization messages generally consist of four categories: (1) racial pride messages: teaching about the positive heritage and history of individuals with African ancestry; (2) preparation for bias messages: highlighting the racial inequalities existing among racial groups and discussing ways to process and cope with experiences of racial discrimination; (3) self-worth messages: emphasizing positive individual traits (e.g., honesty) to help youth develop a positive sense of self; and (4) egalitarian messages: drawing attention to the harmony and equality that can exist among racial groups (Jones and Neblett 756).

Researchers also suggest that the increased visibility of anti-black racial violence in news and social media influences how parents talk to their children (Threlfall 267). For example, in response to George Zimmerman murdering seventeen-year-old Trayvon Martin due to "suspicious behaviour," Anita Thomas and Sha'Kema M. Blackmon found that Black parents believed that young Black boys needed more protection. Participants interpreted the shooting as racialized violence, and Zimmerman's subsequent acquittal left Black families enraged and at a loss across the country (81). Still, we need more acknowledgment of the parental activism of Black mothers and fathers—such as Gina Best (mother of India Kager and member of #SayHerName Mothers Network) and Andrew Grant-Thomas (Black father and cofounder of EmbraceRace)—who elucidate how Black parents historically and currently use their socialization messages and love as politicized care (McClain 48). As we document this period of critical resistance among Black communities, there is a need for scholarship that explicitly considers how Black parents use their experiences, identities, and bodies of knowledge to transmit messages on navigating and subverting racialized violence. In the current chapter, we use a Black feminist approach to consider how Black mothers "understand, question, and challenge contemporary social injustice, like the imposition of deficit-based thinking, white supremacy, and racialized bias in society" (Evans-Winters 15).

The Mothers

We talked to thirty-one Black mothers (twenty-five to fifty-two years old, median age = thirty-five) from across the US (Southeast, n = twelve; Midwest, n = nine; Southwest, n = four; West, n = three; and Northeast, n = three). The women were from diverse racial and ethnic backgrounds, including twenty-four women who identified as African American or Black American, two women who identified as African, one Caribbean American woman, and four biracial Black women. Their household income ranged from $20,000 to more than $150,000 (median = $90,000 to $99,999). Concerning the highest educational attainment, three women had at least some college, eight had earned their bachelor's degree, and twenty had a graduate degree. Most of the women were Christian (n = sixteen), followed by spiritual (n = eleven), and agnostic or atheist (n = four).

Procedures

After obtaining university IRB approval, the principal investigator posted announcements on several social media platforms for Black mothers (e.g., Conscious Parenting for the Culture and Black Mothers of Black Daughters) until we reached the targeted number of mothers (n = thirty) based on available grant funding. Black mothers interested in participating replied to the email to schedule a time for the individual interview with a member of the research team. Given the in-person safety restrictions due to COVID-19, we completed audio interviews through Zoom (a video conferencing platform) or by phone. The interview team consisted of the principal investigator (a Black woman) and two graduate students (a Black woman and Latina woman).

We used a set protocol of questions for each interview, as well as additional probing questions that an interviewer might ask based on the conversation's direction. The interview protocol had four main sections: (1) mothers' disciplinary experiences during childhood; (2) mothers' current parenting practices with their children; (3) mothers' race-related beliefs and experiences; and (4) participants' advice for other Black mothers. In relation to the current study, the most relevant questions included "In what ways do you plan to prepare your children to cope with racism?" and "In the age of social media, we are exposed to frequent stories of police brutality and violence against Black people and communities. To what extent do these stories influence you as a mother? How do you process them?"

Scholarly Positionality

We come to this work as Black feminist mamas and community scholars whose research spans racial equity, intersectionality, educational grassroots organizing, and Black family systems. The first author is a Black woman whose scholarship focusses on the holistic development and cultural resilience of Black girls and women in the context of families, schools, and communities. Her four beautiful children remind her to use storytelling as radical, healing resistance. The second author is a Black woman whose scholarship focuses on anti-blackness, school-community relationships, and educational grassroots organizing. She is a Black mother-bridge-interrupter-scholar who has been a community advocate and organizer since she was twelve. The third author is a Black woman whose scholarship focuses on how social identities, specifically race and gender, along with cultural values systems, like Afro-centric values, influence African American adolescents' social-emotional competencies. Her research is grounded in social and developmental psychology.

Collectively, we believe that Black mothers' perspectives on racialized violence are vital in understanding how we can promote freedom among Black children and radical change within this country. Thus, we drew upon Black feminist qualitative inquiry to guide the analysis. This methodological approach (1) accounts for Black women's historicity as racialized and gendered minorities in the US; (2) involves reflection among scholars and participants to co-construct meaning around their experiences; and (3) situates meaning-making as multidimensional and multilayered. A Black feminist approach allowed us to explore how anti-black racialized violence in the US disrupted the mothers' sense of safety and trust and highlight the profound messages of love and liberation the mothers offered to their children.

Thematic Analysis

We used consensual qualitative research (CQR) methods outlined by Clara E. Hill and Sarah Knox to analyze the data (55). CQR is a thematic form of data analysis that relies on team consensus, believing that multiple informed perspectives render a truer representation of participants' meanings. First, the coding team (three Black women: the lead author and principal investigator and two undergraduate students) reviewed the transcripts and extracted statements discussing such topics as racialized violence, police brutality, racial socialization messages, and the mothers' perspectives on the Black Lives Matter movement. We added the extracted statements to an Excel spreadsheet with four column headings: transcript number, participant response, theme ideas, and additional notes.

After compiling the excerpts, the coding team reviewed all highlighted statements in the Excel file independently and met as a group to identify preliminary coding categories based on themes arising in the data. The lead author and PI explicitly stated that the coding process should be an equitable group effort with input from all members, in which dissenting opinions were welcome and integral to the research process. Our coding dialogues involved broader discussions of state-sanctioned violence and current cases in the news (e.g., Breonna Taylor and George Floyd), as well as our own experiences of racial socialization and racial discrimination. To engage in ongoing reflexivity, we considered our memos about the mothers' excerpts to note our renderings of the interview data. These coding discussions resulted in the final three themes, which we assigned to excerpts within the main coding document. We met weekly to review approximately ten transcripts and discuss disagreements in the coding process. For each disagreement, we returned to the original interview data to reach a consensus.

Findings and Discussion

In line with Black feminist qualitative inquiry, we present each theme with a brief description and then provide first-person accounts from each mother. We hoped this would demonstrate the interiority of their lives by reconstructing the women's knowledge and worldviews on racialized violence as a dehumanizing social ill (Evans-Winters 20). Their words illustrate how Black mothers' activism against oppression on behalf of their children, families, and community, is woven into the fabric of their daily lives (McClain 202).

Theme One

"I See a Lot of Those Stories": Limiting Social Media to Reduce Vicarious Racial Trauma

Over the past few years, more cases of anti-black oppression and racialized violence have been documented (e.g., body cameras and cell phone footage). While this visibility is, in some cases, directly responsible for holding perpetrators accountable for their violence (e.g., Derek Chauvin's murder of George Floyd), it also increases Black individuals' exposure to racially traumatic events and race-based traumatic stress (RBTS). RBTS refers to the mental and emotional injury caused by encounters with racial bias and ethnic discrimination, racism, and hate crimes, including both direct and vicarious experiences (Helms et al. 55). In the first theme, some mothers discussed how they limited their social media and news intake in 2020 to reduce their exposure to racialized violence and the subsequent racial trauma and stress. Angela, a thirty-one-year-old African American mother with four daughters and a son, shared the following:

> During this time, we've literally stopped watching the news. It's just a constant threat of fear every day, and I don't want to instill that into my children at all. I don't want them to be fearful. I want them to be aware but not fearful. We have conversations all the time. We'll sit down and talk with them about things that we feel like is important, but we're just trying to filter what comes in because children watch, they see, they hear all of that. And that can do something to their minds without them even knowing. So trying to make sure that they're not being on overload from all of that. That's my job as a parent I feel.

Although it was important to Angela that she talk with her children about racial injustice and news events, she also believed that it was her job as a parent to limit their exposure to racism. She was concerned about how their exposure to racial violence might contribute to a looming sense of fear, which is one of the many documented health risks (i.e., increased stress, trouble sleeping, anxiety, and depressive symptomology) (Helms et al. 58). Several mothers stated that they had to recognize when it was time for them to turn off the news to prioritize their wellbeing. Claudette, a thirty-one-year-old Jamaican mother with two sons, reflected:

When I view that stuff on social media, I'm viewing it through the lens of a mom whether I realize it or not. I'm viewing it two different ways. What would my kids say if they saw that? How would this affect my kid if they saw that? And then, what do I say to my kid about this? How do I explain this to my kid? It's not as easy to scroll anymore. Everything has a deeper meaning. Even if I decide to keep scrolling and not let it take root in my soul or my heart, I see it. It's there: for me and my kids. So it's like, "Nope. Not going there today." That's a decision I have to make sometimes. To keep my sanity.

Similarly, Gwendolyn a thirty-year-old African American mother with one daughter, said:

Yeah, I have to recognize when it's time to turn things off. That's the biggest thing. Because it can get overwhelming. And there's times where I'm just like, "I don't want her to go anywhere or see anybody or anything." And I'm like, "Okay, that's not realistic." And so it's like, "Well, what tools do I give her to help and process it?" So, I think the first thing that I would want is to talk with my child about them, but also, I have to really process for myself and really monitor and moderate my intake of the news.

Both Claudette and Gwendolyn discussed the importance of protecting their children from too much exposure to racialized violence in the news, and they were particularly mindful of the stress related to witnessing these events. By six years old, children can view media coverage and begin to worry about whether similar events could happen to them and their family (Nationwide Children's Network). While mothers with younger children tended to focus on the messages they would provide to their children in the future, mothers with teenage children discussed how they created the time and space to discuss many of the highly publicized events of 2020 as they happened. Althea, a thirty-eight-year-old African American mother with two daughters and a son, said:

As I mentioned, my oldest is on social media. And we talk about those things, and I have conversations with her about what she has heard and what she has seen. We've talked about a lot of the recent current events. And I have had to remind her, "I know this stuff is heartbreaking. I know it seems like it's a never-ending cycle. At the end of the day, I want you to be aware, and I want you to know what's going on, but I also want you to remember that you're a teenager. These are not things that should consume you just yet. You have plenty of time to carry these burdens. I want you to focus on school, and I want you to focus on your mental health." She gets very involved and sees things on social media, and so I have to remind her, "Take a break. Not everything is meant for you to consume." And I just keep track of what she's looking at.

Althea had to monitor her oldest daughter's social media intake to ensure she was cognizant of the toll it was taking on her daughter's mental health. She mentioned that she reminds her daughter to focus on school and her mental health during this stage in her life because "these are not things that should consume her just yet." The temporal phrasing of her statement suggested that Althea believes that the types of racialized violence that they witnessed in 2020 will continue to occur well into her child's adult life. For many of the mothers, monitoring their children's social media and news intake was a form of protection, consistent with related work on vigilant-involved practices among Black parents (Varner et al. 216). As Charlie, a forty-year-old African American mother with two daughters and a son, noted:

> I think the stories make me more protective in terms of parenting. Just making sure my kids have that sense of discernment, the value of knowing the history. To be safe, but also to understand that you are entitled to your humanity. The purpose of all of this stuff on social media is to terrorize Black people, and the purpose of terrorism is to make people scared so that they move how you want them to move.

Charlie stated that it was important for her children to know their history, which is a common part of Black parents' racial socialization practices. Racial pride and cultural heritage messages provide Black children with a useful lens to process race-related events (Jones and Neblett 759). Finally, mothers noted how the recurring nature of police brutality and state-sanctioned violence in 2020 reminded them of the ubiquity of anti-blackness in the US. Alyce, a thirty-three-year-old biracial (Black and w) mother with one daughter, imparted:

Oh, it can be easy to say, "Oh, well that happened in Wisconsin. We're in Texas. That has nothing to do with us. Oh, that happened to Hispanic people in Los Angeles. That has nothing to do with us in Mississippi." But now social media is saying, "No, no, no." This happens everywhere. I want her to know that just because it happened somewhere else doesn't mean it's not happening in your neighbourhood. Maybe it just looks a little different, or it has a different name, but it's very possible. To be aware so that when you see it coming, you may not know how to approach it, but you know what it looks like, or you know what it sounds like and what could happen from that point forward.

Alyce's words summarized many of the mothers' consciousness on how the events of 2020 were only contemporary manifestations of the long and storied history of anti-black racialized violence in the US. She believed that it was important for her daughter to know that racialized violence "happens everywhere," which aligned well with the excerpts in the second theme about rejecting respectability politics as a necessary component of moving towards Black liberation.

Theme Two

"Do You Mean ALL Black Lives Matter?": Rejecting Respectability Politics as a Pathway to Liberation

Respectability politics refers to a long-standing social and civic debate regarding the idea that Blacks (and other racialized minorities) can minimize or evade discrimination and injustice by behaving—in dress, actions, and speaking—in a "respectable manner" (Obasogie and Newman 541). This debate has played out repeatedly in media coverage after the murder of a Black child or adult (e.g., criticisms on Trayvon Martin's wearing a hoodie, Eric Garner selling loose cigarettes, and Sandra Bland allegedly evading arrest). Yet many of the mothers in our study rebuked the idea that any behaviour or clothing choice could justify state-sanctioned murder. For some mothers, rejecting respectability politics seemed to occur after watching so many instances of police brutality. Henrietta, a twenty-five-year-old African American mother with two daughters, communicated:

It's crushing. Here in St. Louis, in my generation, we have a really strong activist network, and we're going to show up to vote. We're going to show up to hold people accountable and all of that. And it's just a lot of things here in the past couple of years. I think this morning, they released a completely different footage of the George Floyd incident. It was just crushing because the mom in me is like—he's doing all of the steps. He's telling you, "I have anxiety." He's trying to do the countdown to catch his breath. He's trying to lay down and calm his body and you, as a professional, aren't listening. In St. Louis, we just feel like it's one thing after another after another, so we can't even be calm and halfway okay before more bad news comes. It's another video coming out or another case not going to trial. And so it's like, okay we're voting. We're waiting on this process to work its way. We're doing everything y'all told us to do now. You got to give us something.

Similarly, Sylvia, a forty-one-year-old African American mother with two daughters and a son, stated:

We were out with some friends, and they were talking about police brutality. The wife is saying like, "Well, this is why…" Saying Black men need to be clean-cut and don't give them a reason. What world are you in? There is no reason to be treated as inhumane. I said that like, "No, we shouldn't have to change our hairstyles. Your respect for me shouldn't be based on how I speak, this linguistic racism, and linguistic injustice, nothing like that. No, this is just inhumane, and it's unfair. It's violent, and it's anti-black, and there are implications for it." Needless to say, I wasn't invited back to hang out with those folks. The older I get, the more I'm like—good! It is on these structures that are harming us. Even though mothers are trying to protect their daughters or their sons by telling them don't wear the hoodies or don't have your hair looking this way. If you come across the wrong person or the wrong officer, it doesn't matter.

Sylvia described how she called out her friend's wife on the anti-black nature of her argument, as well as her lack of remorse over "not being invited back." She reiterated the shift in her thinking from focusing on individuals' behaviours to systemic problems in policing and justice. Mothers described the myriad emotions they felt in response to hearing about another instance of police brutality in 2020, ranging from sorrow to hopelessness to rage. As Shirlee, a twenty-eight-year-old African American mother with two daughters, shared:

> It hurts too bad; it's too much. I read that another Black person has been slain and murdered, but I stop it at that because I don't want to give an excuse as to why someone wants to.... I don't care if they were actually committing an act of violence or a crime. I don't care if they were minding their business because I don't want to tell my kids, "Make sure you don't do this, this, this, and this." It doesn't matter. I have removed myself from trying to be hip on everything that's going on. I don't want to let that affect the way I parent my child. I don't want to parent out of fear. I'm already scared enough. I don't want to parent specifically out of fear. The best thing I can do is just prepare my kids to keep themselves safe, trust their intuition, and to make good choices. If you don't feel like something is the right thing for you to do, don't do it. But I'm not going to sit here and tell you, "Make sure you're saying 'yes sir,' 'no sir'" because it doesn't matter. If you're going to lose your life, you're going to lose your life.

Shirlee talked about how she limited her engagement with news stories on Black individuals who were murdered because she did not want to read the justifications for their deaths. In addition, she stated that she refused to tell her children that certain mannerisms (e.g., saying "yes sir" and "no sir") would protect them from state-sanctioned violence, since she believed that the responsibility to deescalate a situation rested on police officers rather than lay citizens. In rejecting respectability politics, several mothers encouraged more intersectional forms of organizing within their communities. They wanted to see increased accountability for the racialized violence and harm against all members of the Black community. Daisy, a thirty-nine-year-old African American mother with a daughter, declared:

> A lot of the spaces that I'm in, doing a lot of organizing work ... and some activist spaces are very much I'm like, "What y'all want? Y'all don't want liberation. You want Black male supremacy. That's what you want." I have to be able to call that shit out

and say things to keep spaces safe for me. Because, unfortunately, you have to advocate for yourself many times. I want her [daughter] to know and be able to do that. Because I feel that I do. Even those with the best of intentions, even one of my very good friends, I have to get on him a lot. I said, "Because what about people who are not in the binary? Do you mean all Black lives matter? Because y'all got to be very specific."

Given the disproportionate harm against Black LGTBQ+ individuals (i.e., trans people are 3.7 times more likely to experience police violence and seven times more likely to experience physical violence when interacting with police than cisgender victims and survivors), Daisy made a critical point. In particular, she drew attention to the necessary intra-community work that needed to occur to ensure that those who were especially vulnerable to state-sanctioned violence or who received less structural protection (e.g., Black trans women) (Burns). Daisy stated that she planned to pass these intersectional lessons on to her daughter to ensure that she also learned how to advocate for herself. Similar to Daisy, other mothers discussed how they contextualized racial disparities with their children to encourage them to reject ideologies that maintain respectability politics. Jada, a fifty-year-old Ghanaian mother with two sons, revealed:

> My sons are definitely more aware. They're like, "What we see on social media is definitely upsetting and how do I use my voice to make a change?" I know my younger one sits on panels and does a lot on social justice issues. My older one uses medicine. He's interested in the field of medicine; so he talks about racial issues with healthcare. And really helping their friends understand that they do some of the same things, but they don't have police circulate every day in the neighbourhood ... because if that was the case, it would be very different. A lot of them would have criminal records, right? We helped them understand that the kids they see on TV are not bad kids. We talked a lot about kids in the juvenile justice system, right? They're doing the same thing that is being done in European American homes, but we never apply it to Black and brown kids. So now, my son Miles has done a lot of work on the school-to-prison pipeline and why that exists.

Jada described how she tried to raise her sons to understand how social determinants of health (e.g., conditions in the environments where people live, learn, work, and age that affect a wide range of quality-of-life outcomes and risks) influenced the criminalization of Black and brown children more than white children. She rejected the notion that Black or brown children engaged in more criminal activity and instead highlighted how policing practices contributed to more surveillance and punishment within Black communities. Like Jada, several mothers discussed how they hoped to raise their children with a sense of community care and activism.

Theme Three

"The World Gives Me a Sense of Pain and Purpose": Raising the Next Generation of Freedom Fighters

Another core form of racial socialization is "preparation for bias" (Jones and Neblett 756), which refers to the messages that Black parents provide to their children on racial bias and discrimination. Within the third theme, mothers described how they drew on incidents of anti-black violence and oppression as teachable moments of US history, racism, and power. Many of the mothers connected their daily experiences to the protracted struggles against white supremacy and state-sanctioned violence within the Black community, and they were intentional about when and how they talked about these topics with their children. Miriam, a forty-two-year-old Black American mother with two sons, stated:

> I don't have these conversations with my four-year-old because he's four years old. The older child ... we talk about it. We also try to focus on what we can do to make things better. I'm not that big on marching, but can we leverage our economic dollars? Can we be effective by voting on laws and talking to our friends about what's going on? I think he's still somewhat removed from it because he hasn't had that experience. Maybe he will, and maybe he won't. But we tend to focus on what he can do. Because if he is focusing on the negative, it's only going to make him feel helpless and hopeless.

Likewise, Maya, a fifty-year-old African American mother with one son, expressed:

> We've got a standing weekly phone call where we talk about this type of stuff. We practise what to do if the police pull you over. Where do you put your hands? What do you say? Whenever I'm pulled over by the police. and he's in the car with me ... before I drive off, I ask, "How do you feel?" What did you see the cops were doing? What did you see me doing? Even now, I teach him that racism is part of life and regardless of how it impacts him, he has to keep going. I tell him: You can go around it. You can go under it, through it, between it, but you keep going."

It was important to Miriam and Maya that they talk with their children about the various ways to participate in civic engagement (e.g., voting and talking with friends). In addition, they wanted their children to understand that while racism was a common experience for Black Americans in the US, they did not have to possess a sense of helplessness or hopelessness. Within their messages on civic participation and interacting with police, the mothers were shaping their children's perspectives on their right to take up space and have a sense of agency. For some mothers, raising the next generation of freedom fighters was about helping their children learn to live their truth and find joy in their existence. Daisy, a thirty-nine-year-old African American mother with a daughter, shared:

> I know the truth of it is that we're not safe in this world. But I still have to find joy, and I still have to find happiness, and take each day and do the best I can. That's what I want her to do. I don't want her anxiety to be like mine because I get so overwhelmed. What about this, this, and this? Because I can't control shit. I can't control how police are going to engage her. But I want her to be able to love herself, find joy, and live.

The mothers were well aware that racial discrimination and anti-black oppression were widespread and could affect themselves and their children. Still, when faced with day-to-day media saturated with violence against Black bodies, they recognized that joy and love go a long way. In a hauntingly beautiful statement that summed up the mothers' thoughts and feelings, Fannie, a thirty-nine-year-old African American mother with a daughter and a son, said:

Did that help Trayvon? Did that help Philando? Did that help George? All these people were compliant. All these people did all the things that you wanted them to do, right? Every one of them had a parent who gave them the speech about do this and do that. And they're all dead, so what the fuck? If that model worked, I would go with it. If it kept me alive and kept people like me alive, I would sacrifice my beliefs for that. Sandra's ass didn't put her turn signal on and ended up dead. So how about this? They're going to have to work for it. You're going to have to work to kill me. I am not going to lay down and let you kill me ... and that is how I want my children to live and breathe. I think it was Zora Neale Hurston who said, "They'll kill you and say that you enjoyed it," right? When I was pregnant with my daughter ... all these Black people died, and all I could think about was I have to raise you to live and survive and be better. Maybe she's going to change the world by living her best life, so I wanted to cultivate that best life. Being free. Being independent. Being happy. Being all the things and none of the things. Having all the choices. I know that she is going to change the world.

Conclusion

In this chapter, we privileged the voices and lived experiences of Black mothers regarding their decision-making on discussing racialized violence and social inequality with their children. Our findings revealed that Black mothers feel a tremendous responsibility when thinking about their children's potential encounters with police officers in the US. They reminded us that it is critical that we focus less on Black individuals' behaviours and potential success in deescalating officers and instead focus on dismantling policies and practices that support anti-black police violence (Smith 37). Their narratives advance the sparse literature on Black family processes during a pivotal period of Black community resistance and protest and uplift Black parenting as cultural resilience against anti-black state-sanctioned violence.

Works Cited

Anderson, Riana, et al. "The Initial Development and Validation of the Racial Socialization Competency Scale: Quality and Quantity." *Cultural Diversity and Ethnic Minority Psychology*, vol. 26, no. 4, 2020, pp. 426–36.

Burns, Katelyn. "Why Police Often Single Out Trans People for Violence." *Vox*, 23 June 2020, https://www.vox.com/identities/2020/6/23/21295432/police-black-trans-people-violence. Accessed 28 Dec. 2024.

Cooper, Shauna, et al. "That Is Why We Raise Children": African American Fathers' Race-Related Concerns for Their Adolescents and Parenting Strategies." *Journal of Adolescence*, vol. 82, 2020, pp. 67–81.

Evans-Winters, Venus E. *Black Feminism in Qualitative Inquiry: A Mosaic for Writing Our Daughter's Body*. Routledge Press, 2019.

Hill, Clara E., and Sarah Knox. *Essentials of Consensual Qualitative Research*. American Psychological Association, 2021.

Jones, Shawn, and Enrique Neblett. "Future Directions in Research on Racism-Related Stress and Racial-Ethnic Protective Factors for Black Youth." *Journal of Clinical Child & Adolescent Psychology*, vol. 46, no. 5, 2017, pp. 754–66.

McClain, Danielle. *We Live for the We: The Political Power of Black Motherhood*. Bold Type Books, 2019.

Mouzon, Dawne, et al. "Discrimination and Psychiatric Disorders among Older African Americans." *International Journal of Geriatric Psychiatry*, vol. 32, no. 2, 2017, pp. 175–82.

Obasogie, Osagie K., and Zachary Newman. "Black Lives Matter and Respectability Politics in Local News Accounts of Officer-Involved Civilian Deaths: An Early Empirical Assessment." *Wisconsin Law Review*, no. 3, 2016, pp. 541–74.

Nationwide Children's Network. "Caring for Children After Exposure to Race-Related Violence in the Media." Nationwide Children's Network, 3 June 2020, https://www.nationwidechildrens.org/. Accessed 28 Dec. 2024.

Smith, Christen A. "Facing the Dragon: Black Mothering, Sequelae, and Gendered Necropolitics in the Americas." *Journal of the Association of Black Anthropologists*, vol. 24, no. 1, 2016, pp. 31–48.

Story, Kaila A. "Mama's Gon' Buy You a Mockingbird: Why #Black MothersStillMatter: A Short Genealogy of Black Mothers' Maternal Activism and Politicized Care." *Biography*, vol. 41, no. 4, 2018, pp. 876–94.

Thomas, Anita, and Sha'Kema MBlackmon. "The Influence of the Trayvon Martin Shooting on Racial Socialization Practices of African American Parents." *Journal of Black Psychology*, vol. 41, no. 1, 2015, pp. 75–89.

Threlfall, Jennifer M. "Parenting in the Shadow of Ferguson: Racial Socialization Practices in Context." *Youth & Society*, vol. 50, no. 2, pp. 255–73.

Varner, Fatima, et al. "Dealing with Discrimination: Parents' and Adolescents' Racial Discrimination Experiences and Parenting in African American Families." *Cultural Diversity and Ethnic Minority Psychology*, vol. 26, no. 2, 2020, pp. 215–20.

23.

The Judicialization of Black Suffering: Black Motherhood and the Criminal Justice System in Rio de Janeiro, Brazil

Luciane Rocha

On the night of November 25, 2015, four military police officers shot seven young Black men in Barros Filho, an economically poor neighbourhood in the northern part of Rio de Janeiro. Five of the young men, who were in the car that was hit 111 times, died on the spot; two other young men who were on a motorcycle survived. The police officers were arrested, and the Public Prosecutor's Office charged them with five counts of intentional homicide with three aggravated offences and two counts of attempted homicide, in addition to the crimes of procedural fraud and illegal possession of a firearm with the serial number removed. The families of the young men were assisted by the Human Rights Center of the Public Defender's Office of Rio de Janeiro to monitor the progress of the criminal justice system and to open a civil lawsuit for compensation.[1]

Months later, on July 4, 2016, the third hearing for the investigation into the killing, which became known as the Costa Barros Massacre, took place. To increase visibility and political pressure, family members, mainly members, of this and other crimes committed by police officers organized a demonstration in front of the Court of Justice in Rio de

Janeiro. During the more than three hours of protest, the mothers took turns at the microphone as people passed by. As they recalled the deaths of their sons and daughters, they gave testimony about the terror and violence perpetuated by the state,[2] exchanged experiences about their interactions with the criminal justice system and, most importantly, showed solidarity through their common experience of Black suffering. During this demonstration, Luiza,[3] one of the mothers, said:

> My son was Black, young, poor and from the favelas, but he had his dreams, which were interrupted by these police officers, these murderers. Police officers who were supposed to defend us ended my son's life, but not only his. They ended mine and my family's. I was living on medication, depressed. I left work.... I have three more daughters. I went from my mourning to the fight.... My son was only seventeen years old when he was murdered. They are there to defend us, and they kill us. The bullet that killed my son was not free; it was paid for with my sweat ... the blood of our children spilled. We want justice! Not their justice, which comes killing and dishonouring us, calling us all kinds of names. We are mothers and relatives of victims of this state. We want justice, public health and schools for our children to study.

Luiza's speech reveals several aspects of the "mothers' war" (Farias and Vianna) and "outraged motherhood" (Rocha): highlighting the intersectionality of race, class, age, and place of residence; naming the state as the oppressor; demanding social transformations; highlighting physical, financial, and emotional consequences caused by death; and, above all, demanding justice. These aspects show the importance of public acts before the Court of Justice and other criminal justice institutions.

When Luiza finished her speech, the other mothers exclaimed: "The dead have a voice!" This is an expression used by mothers of victims of police violence in Brazil as a way of affirming the continuity of motherhood, even after the violent, cruel, and preventable death of their sons and daughters (Carvalho). Giving voice to the dead entails a paradigm shift, in which instead of silence and the usual withdrawal for mourning, mothers use their pain politically. They confront society by exposing Black suffering and denouncing death. It is through this outraged mourning that they question the precariousness of Black lives and refuse the gradual disappearance of the pain caused by death, thus avoiding the fog of oblivion. It is the pain of absence that incites them to fight for the necessary structural changes in society and demand justice.

In this chapter, I analyze the work of the Human Rights Defence Centre of the Rio de Janeiro Public Defender's Office (NUDEDH) in cases in which family members of victims of police violence, especially mothers, play a relevant role in moving the criminal justice system's procedures. Based on participant observation at the NUDEDH, judicial hearings, and trials between 2015 and 2017, in this chapter, I analyze the uses of Black suffering in the criminal justice system through the following questions. How does the criminal justice system listen to the voices of mothers of victims of violence? How important are the mothers' narratives for the racial debate in the criminal justice system? What political and legal tools do they activate before the hearings and trials? The chapter is divided into two parts. First, I outline the methodology used to investigate Black suffering in the judicial system through the Public Defender's Office. In the second section, I analyze three legal cases of violence committed by the state and assisted by NUDEDH through critical race theory.

Investigating the Public Defender's Office

Researchers Klarissa Silva and Ludmila Ribeiro define the criminal justice system in Brazil as "the articulation of police organizations, the Public Prosecutor's Office, the Public Defender's Office, the Judiciary and the Penitentiary System, with the objective of facilitating the processing of conflicts classified as offenses (crimes or misdemeanors) in the country's existing criminal laws" (15). Texts analyzing the role of the Public Defender's Office in the criminal justice system define it as a fundamental institution for democracy and for guaranteeing human rights (Roig; Sadek).[4] The Public Defender's Office works to promote the balance of inequalities in order to punish those who are "above" the law and the constitution, and defend those who are "below", thus seeking greater symmetry between those differentiated by color, economic, political, cultural, corporate or bureaucratic reasons.

The most visible aspect of the Black genocide in Brazil[5] is the murder of poor young men, but it also manifests itself in the suffering of thousands of mothers, fathers, family members, and communities. Each life lost brings pain, deeply penetrating the network of relatives and friends of those murdered, but it especially affects the lives of mothers, who are often the main breadwinners of the family. They are the ones directly affected by this violence and the ones who are on the frontlines demanding justice. It is precisely these mothers' experiences of pain and resistance that I focus on in this study.

From a partnership previously established with a network of family members of victims of violence,[6] I identified among these family members those whom the Public Defender's Office assisted. Once the first two families were identified, preliminary interviews were conducted about the role of this institution in their cases. The objective of the interviews with the family members was to develop a strategy for approaching the Public Defender's Office. I found that the families were not aware of the work of these legal professionals until they were approached by them offering assistance in their cases. Family members of victims of police violence were assisted by the Human Rights Defence Centre of the Public Defender's Office—NUDEDH.

The coordinator of the mothers' network at the time gave me the telephone number of NUDEDH's coordinator, and I was soon able to schedule a meeting to be introduced to the centre's programs. I identified that the Human Rights Defence Program was the one that works on unsolved homicide cases and therefore the ideal place to develop the study on the flow of the criminal justice system. After a formal request to conduct the research, the coordinator sent his approval to the Public Defender General, who authorized my access to the NUDEDH's activities for qualitative and quantitative analysis.

I began the archival research by consulting active procedures. I read the procedures to identify the rules guiding the professional practices of public defenders and their main interlocutors: civil police, public hospital directors, forensic medical institute (IML) employees, and the family members themselves. In addition to this procedural study, I examined the meetings between defenders and the mothers, followed the cases assisted by NUDEDH, observed and documented the public events organized by mothers of victims of violence, and conducted interviews with public defenders and family members.

The Human Rights Unit of the Rio de Janeiro Public Defender's Office divides its activities into ten programs.[7] Among them, the program with the largest number of cases during the period of this investigation was the program called Victims of Human Rights Violations. This program had 285 cases when I began fieldwork in January 2016, rising to 309 in July 2017, when I finished the ethnography. Of the 285 cases I analyzed in July 2016, 126 referred to events involving a state agent. I found that in eighteen cases, the Public Defender's Office acted as an assistant to the prosecution.[8] This is an important window of investigation that has not yet been explored in the Brazilian literature.

Article 288 of the Brazilian Code of Criminal Procedure states the assistant to the prosecution is the victim, his ascendant or sibling, but in any case, he needs a lawyer to file a claim in court. It is common for the Public Defender's Office to act as the institution responsible for the defence of defendants in criminal proceedings to guarantee comprehensive legal assistance, as well as broad and full defence. In cases where the Public Defender's Office is sought to act criminally in favour of the victim, and the interested party does not have the financial capacity to hire him, the Public Defender must qualify as an assistant to the prosecution, acting alongside the Public Prosecutor's Office in the jury room, sometimes opposite another public defender who will act in defence of the defendant.

NUDEDH has acted as an assistant to the prosecution mainly in cases of homicide committed by police officers resulting from stray bullets or confrontations in favelas.[9] In this sense, the Public Defender's Office has begun to occupy a space in the legal-political-media scenario, with the defender being repeatedly invited to give interviews to newspapers and participate in documentaries and events organized by community leaders. In this investigation, due to the hearing schedule, I was able to follow the work of the NUDEDH defenders authorized as legal representatives in three cases: Eduardo de Jesus, Costa Barros Case, and Johnatha Oliveira Case.

Public defender Jorge Empathy[10] stated the following about the importance of acting as a prosecutor's assistant:

> The defence attorney ends up being the closest to the families in the justice system. As assistants to the prosecution, we have to demonstrate, we have to prove in court, what happened and how it happened because the first narrative is that of the police officers. We also demonstrate the consequences of the event for the family because this can have an impact on the sentencing. The severity, peculiarities, circumstances, etc. and already anticipating what the defence's argument will be: they always argue that the young

Black men are criminals, therefore, justifying the killing. They will say that some of the victims had a police record; this is used to acquit the police officer because Black death is already very naturalized, so it automatically makes the death legitimate. So ... the judge is not the one who will judge; it is the popular jury, and we never know who will be there. They will also say that they reacted to the violence against them, that it is a conflict zone, etc., so it is important for us to prove what really happened.

To prove these circumstances, the defender studies all the documents produced by the criminal justice system in the aforementioned process: police report, police investigation, and complaint (Varga). Defender Luiz Honesty said: "We try to find contradictions between the statements of the defendants and defence witnesses, we compare them with the technical evidence, we try to find loopholes to denaturalize racial stereotypes that justify the crime, and, above all, we inform the victims' families about what happened."

On the days of the hearings, especially on days when prosecution witnesses testify, the defence attorney informs the family members of what is expected to happen, preparing them for the suffering that will be required in court. After the hearing, he talks to the family members while they are still inside the Court of Justice to share his first impressions of the session and the next steps. In some cases, the NUDEDH schedules a meeting with the family members to answer further questions. In what follows, I present the theoretical framework for analyzing the work of the Defence Office in collaboration with the mothers.

Case Studies: Black Suffering and the Judicial System

Critical race theory is a broad theoretical framework that emerged around 1989 as a reaction against the critical legal studies (CLS) movement due to the latter's failure to recognize how race is a central component of the very systems of law it contests. CRT is also informed by feminist thought, bringing together issues such as gender, whiteness, and racism to address power imbalances.

Since the 1990s, CRT has increased in reach and popularity, providing the intellectual and methodological foundations for work in legal scholarship and across a range of social sciences (Graham; Zuberi). Simply put, CRT is concerned with how the state creates and perpetuates race and racism. For example, Eduardo Bonilla-Silva offers a "structural interpretation" of racism that accounts for "racialized social systems." Similarly, Joe Feagin demonstrates how the American state was founded to promote white supremacy and traces the effects of systemic racism to the present day.

Although CRT initially focussed on the United States (US), its insights are also pertinent to Brazil (Rocha). In the American context, CRT complements and extends the sociological production of race by specifying and analyzing racist premises and structures in legal institutions and written laws that institutionalize white supremacy. CRT, therefore, provides an improved analysis of the processes and rules that form the backbone of the State and racial inequality. In Brazil, Thula Pires and Caroline Lyrio discuss how the law represents and reproduces the dynamics of oppression. According to the authors, CRT allows "the possibility of the criterion of race [to be] used as a privileged lens for analyzing this reality" (62).

The first premise asserts that racism is a central, permanent, and normal part of society (Solórzano and Delgado; Stefancic). As Delgado Bernal (2002) states, "Because racism is an ingrained feature, it seems common and natural to people in society" (xvi). Edward Taylor asserts that "assumptions of White superiority are so embedded in political, legal, and educational structures that they are almost unrecognizable [and] because racism is pervasive and ubiquitous, it cannot easily be recognized by its beneficiaries" (73–74). Ironically, the result is that whites cannot see or understand the world they have created and, in many cases, are quick to dismiss or deny the inherited privilege associated with whiteness.

Derrick Bell states that racism "is at the core, not at the periphery; in the permanent, not the fleeting; in the real lives of ... non-White and White people" (198). However, Black people have experiential knowledge of living under such systems of racism and oppression and have thus developed methodologies that serve as coping mechanisms and as ways to raise awareness of issues that affect them and that are often overlooked and unconsidered.

The second premise of CRT lies in its commitment to the centrality of experiential knowledge, as detailed through the use of narratives (Solórzano and Delgado Bernal; Delgado and Stefancic). Because white people do not always recognize or understand the experiences of people of colour, CRT developed the methodology of counternarratives to relate to the racial realities of nonwhite people while providing opportunities for people of colour to challenge myths, assumptions, and received wisdom.

The use of narrative in CRT recognizes the experiential knowledge of the nondominant as "legitimate, appropriate, and critical for understanding and analyzing racial subordination" (Solórzano and Delgado Bernal 314). A CRT scholar uses these narratives with a deep commitment to social justice and the elimination of racial discrimination as part of the broader goal of ending all forms of oppression (Dixson and Rousseau 4).

Johnatha Oliveira Case: The Challenge of Dominant Ideologies, Motherhood, and Moral Evidence

> When my son died, I couldn't believe it. I went into a kind of coma. I couldn't eat. I couldn't get out of bed. One day, I managed to get up and watch TV. When the news came on, they talked about my son's case and said that he was "supposedly involved in drug trafficking." They talked about it at the end, right after showing the people's protest. Right at the end, as if to say that he was just another unimportant person. That made me indignant. The next day I gathered my things and went to seek justice for my son.

This is how Ana Paula Oliveira, mother of Johnatha Oliveira, recounts how she began her search for justice. Like many mothers who transform their grief into a political struggle, Ana Paula transformed her indignation at the normalization of her son's death into fuel to emerge from her social coma, became a protagonist in moving the criminal justice steps into a solution, and became an activist against police violence in Rio de Janeiro. Her struggle is related to a fundamental aspect of the CRT: challenging the dominant ideology. Before the now common dissemination of fake news that associates people who were murdered in favelas with crime, the media already tried to justify these deaths by using such phrases as "he had a history in the system" or "he was a possible drug dealer." In the favelas, life is dehumanized, and death is naturalized.

In this sense, Ana Paula's political struggle is fundamentally about denaturalizing these narratives, since the criminalization of young people, especially young Black people, is also transferable to mothers as they continue to manage their motherhood within the criminal justice system. Ana Paula said in an interview that she would not "allow herself to be called the mother of criminals—a category that also criminalizes them—and that the real criminals will be held accountable." She states: "It is not just the police officer who pulled the trigger who must be held accountable. The governor, the secretary of public security and the entire judiciary have their hands dirty with the blood of my son, and of all the other young people and children who are being exterminated."

Johnatha Oliveira was murdered by military police officers in May 2014. He was shot in the back while returning from his girlfriend's house in the Manguinhos favela. He was assisted by residents but arrived dead at the local emergency care unit. When analyzing the case procedure at NUDEDH, I found that during the police investigation, the police officers claimed the following: "They were advancing through the favela in search of a drug den when they heard gunshots and fired back. They were immediately surprised by the protest of residents who threw stones at them and retreated, not seeing if there were any injuries." They also stated that they had recognized Johnatha "from his involvement in local crime."

Ana Paula's work to obtain justice for her son's death involved presenting moral evidence about him that discredits the narrative that her son was a criminal. To this end, she was called as a witness to talk about his life, countering the image created by the police, and the public defender qualified as an assistant to the prosecution so that, according to him, he could "ask her the right questions." This case can also be analyzed through another aspect of CRT: counternarratives. In CRT, storytelling is powerful because it reveals the racist acts that people face daily, challenging the universally held beliefs of the majority. Interpreting the experience of racism differs based on the degree of power and authority a person has in society. In this sense, these stories and lived experiences need to be told, heard, and analyzed to understand how racism operates in the criminal justice system.

According to Empathy, NUDEDH quickly followed up on this case. He attributes this speed to the visibility of the case due to Ana Paula's activism, who called on residents and NGOs to help put pressure on the system. Ana Paula had this to say:

> In addition to being very nervous because I had never set foot in a court of law, I didn't know how to act. My son's killer was there, and it was the first time I had seen him. The hearing was scheduled

for 1:00 p.m. and didn't start until 6:00 p.m. I was very afraid that the witnesses would leave. I had to work hard to persuade and be kind to people so they would stay with me. It was everyone's first time in that building. At the first hearing, I wasn't with the Public Defender's Office yet, but with a volunteer lawyer. A victim's mother recommended the change and he helped a lot. At the other hearings, I went with the defender and felt safer because they were experts in the criminal area. I knew it would be very difficult to take action against the state, so I looked for my best option because they have a team that is very open to helping and they do a good job. I continued to take care of my son even after he was dead. We know that this system is racist. I know that if Johnatha hadn't been a young Black man living in a favela, he wouldn't even be a target of the police. I fulfilled my role as a mother before and after his death.

Fundamental to Ana Paula's actions were the political demonstrations she organized before each hearing and the preservation of her son's memory through the photos shared on her social networks. Her activism was not limited to the criminal justice system. Ana Paula exhibited photos from the beginning of Johnatha's life. These exhibitions demonstrate a dynamic mothers use in the fight against the state. First, they need to show the state and society that their children were loved and that they were good mothers. Second, mothers need to reveal the cruel nature of the death and convey their suffering to the judge and the court. Finally, they need to validate their demands and struggle.

Part of Ana Paula's strategy was to use photos of birthday parties, baptisms, and outings with family. These photos worked to construct counternarratives aiming to show that her son was a good person and was loved. This narrative of affection and longing is also documented in the criminal justice system. Her statement read as follows: "He was at home when he received a message from his aunt asking him to come to her house because she had made his favourite dessert. He jumped up and grabbed his mother and left for his aunt's house, then stopped by his girlfriend's house." She also forwarded newspaper reports about her struggle to the Public Defender's Office, which shows that she did not give up fighting for her son. Her suffering was visible, pressing, and moving.

This mobilization produced enough evidence for this case to be sent to a jury trial. As Ana Paula said, "For me, justice has been served every day that I speak out and manage to bring another mother from the favela together. They look to me for guidance so that their children's cases do not go unpunished."

CRT also challenges dominant assertions of race neutrality, equality of opportunity, objectivity, colour blindness, and merit (Dixson and Rousseau). It questions the dominant ideology and the "racial ideological paradigms that act as camouflage for the self-interest, power, and privilege of dominant groups in society" (Solórzano and Delgado Bernal 313). This self-interest has been most notably discussed through the development of interest convergence theory, which holds that "White elites will tolerate or encourage racial advances in justice only when such advances also advance the White interest" (Bell xvii)—that is, their own interests.

Eduardo de Jesus Case: Principle of Convergence of Interest and the Importance of Technical Evidence

The result of the police investigation and the decision of the judges regarding the death of the ten-year-old Eduardo de Jesus—which occurred on April 2, 2015, in the Complexo do Alemão in the city of Rio de Janeiro—can be analyzed based on the premise of the convergence of interests of the CRT. Teresinha de Jesus, Eduardo's mother told me in an interview that there was no confrontation at the time her son was killed. He was sitting in front of the house waiting for his sister and playing with his cell phone. Teresinha heard a loud noise, ran to the sidewalk, and saw the police trying to modify the crime scene by removing her son's body, which the arrival of her family and neighbours stopped. For her efforts, a rifle was pointed at her and she was threatened with death.

The Civil Police Homicide Division excused the actions of the military police officers by claiming that they had been fighting with drug traffickers and had missed with gunfire. However, a report attached to the case proceedings at the NUDEDH shows that the crime took place in broad daylight and that the police officers were about five meters away from Eduardo. This fact reiterates the perception that in the favelas, the state of exception (Agamben) is normalized and deaths are legitimized.

On November 29, 2016, I conducted participant observation at the Plenary Session of Justices of the Second Criminal Chamber of the Court of Justice, which ended up archiving Eduardo de Jesus's case. A sheet on the door listed the cases that would be analyzed in the session and their order. The case of Eduardo's murder was third on the list. The session was delayed by an hour, and we met—Eduardo's mother, defender, supporters and researchers—in a parallel hallway because there were uniformed police officers at the room's door and Eduardo's mother did not want to stay there.

The defence attorney tried to calm Terezinha down and told those present that the day before he had spoken with one of the judges who he believed would be more receptive to his request to vote against the archiving of the case. According to the defence attorney, "Since he is more experienced than the other, if he votes first, he may also convince the other judge who still has to vote, but you never know. He assured them that his understanding was not to archiving the case."

The judge favoured the defence's request to dismiss the case. According to her, the judges "had a duty to dismiss the case to send a message to the police officers that they can perform their duties without being criminalized." In addition to this argument, she considered the ineptitude of the prosecution and the lack of evidence to continue the case, since the investigation by the Homicide Division did not indicate which police officer fired the shot that killed Eduardo. The second judge voted without much hesitation: "I am in favour of the rapporteur's understanding." The third judge considered the decision "extreme and premature," but he was the dissenting voice. "There was legitimate cowardice, not legitimate defence," said Terezinha de Jesus, with tears in her eyes as she left the room.

Through the principle of convergence of interests, it is possible to understand that if the case was refused to be shelved without identifying the police officer who killed Eduardo, it would open up case law for holding the state responsible for other deaths that occur in favelas without identifying the shooting police officer. Acting in a protective manner of its interests, the state, through the Second Criminal Chamber, decided to maintain the interests of the elite and shelve the case, thus sending a message not only to the police officers that "they can perform their duties without being criminalized" but also to Black and poor people that the criminal justice system does not care about their suffering.

The public defender who is following the case raised the possibility of trying to reverse the annulment in the Superior Court of Justice. To achieve this, political mobilization is essential to ensure the case is not forgotten. This case shows that it is essential that marginalized populations demand the preservation of the crime scene, an on-site expert report, and a thorough investigation by the civil police. Despite all the despair and suffering caused by the death of a loved one, it is essential to understand that the state is not impartial and that it is up to the bereaved to pressure the criminal justice system to work in their favour.

Because challenging the dominant ideology is a daunting undertaking, CRT scholars use an interdisciplinary perspective, which challenges the "historical requirement for the unidisciplinary focus of most analyses" by "analyzing race and racism [and] placing them in a historical and contemporary context using interdisciplinary methods" (Solórzano and Delgado Bernal 314).

Gender and feminist analyses are fundamental concepts in CRT. Kimberlé Crenshaw (1995), Cheryl Harris (1995), Dorothy E. Roberts (1995), Linda Greene (1995), and others have provided a Black feminist discourse to this theory. Crenshaw introduced intersectionality to demonstrate how race, class, gender, sexual identity, marital status, citizenship status, and other social identities often serve as points of marginality and influence the criminal justice system. Several scholarly works employ Crenshaw's analytical intervention to examine and understand the persistent inequality affecting women (McCall; Nash).

In this last case study, I would like to propose a link between theorizations of Black suffering and CRT. Frank Wilderson III states that narrative cannot express the experience of Black suffering without subjecting this experience to structural adjustment. In other words, it is necessary to transcribe this suffering into something tangible for non-Black people. When analyzing the attempt to communicate Black suffering during slavery, Saidiya Hartman explains that "Black sentience [the ability to feel] is inconceivable and unimaginable, but in the very ease of possessing the humiliated and enslaved body, it ultimately elides the understanding and recognition of the slave's pain" (19). In other words, the need to communicate Black pain to and/or through the white body eliminates the possibility of understanding Black pain.

Costa Barros Case: Counternarrative and the Judicialization of Emotions

Wilton, Wilkerson, Lourival, Wesley, Cleiton, Carlos Eduardo, and Roberto, aged between sixteen and thirty, are the seven young Black men who were the victims of the Costa Barros case. However, it is also possible to include as the secondary victims Joselita de Souza, Roberto's mother, who died due to a sudden illness resulting from her depression.

In the police report, the police allege that there was a shootout and that the victims found themselves between the police and the drug dealers. However, witnesses in the case, including the two survivors and other relatives of the victims, contradicted that account and reported that the police shot the young men as soon as they turned the corner without even asking them to stop for questioning. The police officers were arrested the day after the incident for homicide and procedural fraud. For a while, they remained free during the trial, but in November 2019, they were sentenced to fifty-two years in prison by a jury.

NUDEDH became involved in the case shortly after the burial of the young men. The public defenders approached the victims' families to offer assistance in the case. During my research at NUDEDH, I found that four preparatory meetings were held between the defenders and the families and that three evidentiary hearings were held at the Court of Justice.

CRT allows for the analysis of the defence and prosecution of the accused. The complaint filed by the Prosecutor's Office considers, among other issues, that "the crimes were committed for a despicable reason, since the accused shot the victims because they believed that they were involved in the crime and, for this reason, could kill them." The defence attorneys indicate through the questions asked during the hearings that they built their arguments based on the crime that existed near the crime scene and the lack of preparation of the police officers involved. However, for the defence attorneys, as well as for the family members interviewed, what made this occurrence, and the resulting fraud possible, was the case involved the deaths of five poor Black youths. According to Empathy,

> This is an indefensible case, and the role of the Public Defender's Office assisting the prosecution is much more to prove in court the damage caused to the family and to hold the state accountable for normalizing the deaths of young Black men. The boys were

passing by; the police did not give them the order to stop and started shooting at them like crazy. But something went wrong. They tried to fake a crime scene by placing a gun on them. The time it took them to do the simulation drew a lot of attention.... There were many witnesses, and there was pressure from society to hold them accountable. And this started with the police officer on duty who arrested them. They were arrested in the act. People found gloves and other things. People voluntarily went to the police station to speak up. All of these things make the case different ... Different from the case that happened last week in Acari. It was a brutal and faked death, but the boy was really involved in drug trafficking. Unfortunately, this has become so commonplace that the family ended up withdrawing the complaint. There is also something that affects the [criminal justice system] ... vulnerability, people's fear of speaking. This makes a big difference.

In fact, since this case is considered indefensible, proposing out-of-court pension agreements and granting interviews to formal and alternative media have been two important activities of the case's defenders. Empathy continues:

We have a protocol with them [State Attorney's Office]. An agreement. This month we're even going to formalize it because it's something we already do. We already know that judicial agreements are much faster than legal proceedings. Legal proceedings with the state necessarily take many years. Sometimes up to ten years because they take them to the last instance and then there's the court order. So we make the agreement and continue with the criminal proceedings. And so we make an immediate reparation— that is, as quickly as we can. Could they earn more? Maybe they could. Could they earn less? That's fine. They might not even win. But they would certainly know about it much later.

Another role of the Public Defender's Office in the case has been to manage failures in the criminal justice system. An example of this was the revocation of the preventive detention of the police officers, which according to the defender was due to a failure in the "argumentation of the judge [who is responsible for the case in Rio de Janeiro] and the defence clung to this loophole." However, the judge had "already denied this request for freedom several times with well-founded decisions."

Witnesses used stories and evidence of racial violence in the Costa Barros case. One of the mothers narrated:

> My son wanted to serve in the navy, and he was executed inside a car with 111 shots. They ended my son's life, and then they ended mine, too, because I couldn't even get out of bed. I thank my ex-husband who took care of my daughter because I couldn't even get up. When I opened my eyes, I felt sadness in my soul knowing that my son was machine-gunned without doing anything.

For Empathy, these narratives are important to help raise awareness among the jury. However, emotion is rationalized and judicialized. Once the story is told, the examination of the key elements of the story must be based on legal principles, propositions, and arguments. CRT says that this analysis must also be based on representation as a form of critical legal analysis.

In summary, CRT argues racism is a central part of society; it challenges dominant assertions of racial neutrality, equal opportunities, objectivity, colour blindness, and merit and adopts an interdisciplinary and intersectional perspective. I believe that these theoretical and methodological contributions are fundamental to the study of unsolved violent deaths and Black suffering in the Brazilian criminal justice system.

In this chapter, I sought to reflect on the ways in which criminal justice system responds to Black suffering expressed in the narratives of mothers of victims of police violence and on this violence's importance in the system's functioning. To this end, I investigated three cases in which family members played an important role in making the cases visible and acted as assistants to the prosecution in partnership with the Human Rights Defence Centre of the Public Defender's Office of Rio de Janeiro. Applying CRT to analyze the cases, I showed that what happens in this partnership is the judicialization of Black suffering in an attempt to communicate Black pain and challenge the structural, gratuitous, and expected violence against these bodies. However, these cases were unsuccessful. In the three cases studied in this paper, the police officers who murdered the Black youth were acquitted. As Terezinha said, "They don't care about our suffering."

Endnotes

1. This ethnography was carried out for the research project "Determinants of Unsolved Violent Deaths: Flow of Registration, Investigation, Clarification, Reporting and Judgment of Violent Deaths in the City of Rio de Janeiro."
2. Joao Vargas addresses the political and analytical gain of approaching state violence against Black bodies as a genocidal continuum.
3. This is a fictitious name and pays homage to Luiza Mahin, a Black leader who turned her home into the headquarters of the main Black revolts that occurred in Salvador in the mid-nineteenth century. She participated in the Great Insurrection of 1835, the Malê Revolt, the last major slave revolt that occurred in the city.
4. In a review of studies on the criminal justice system, the following stand out: Adorno; Cano; Kant de Lima; Oliveira and Machado; Rifiotis et al.; Sapori; Vargas; Vargas and Rodrigues; Vianna.
5. Black genocide is understood as the denial—physical, cultural, symbolic—to members of Black communities in the African diaspora of the right to survive fully as full citizens or human beings (Nascimento; Vargas).
6. I am referring to the Network of Communities and Movements Against Violence, which was formed in 2004 as a result of the organized struggle of communities and social movements against state violence.
7. Below, I list the programs and the number of active cases in July 2017: public civil action (77); international advocacy (16); biolaw (8); citizen has a name and surname (16); defence of socially vulnerable groups (85); human rights of state agents (7); international refugee law (11); intersectoral exchange (50); prison monitoring (65); and victims of human rights violation (309).
8. There are ten other cases in which the Public Defender's Office acts as a supporter of the prosecution in other matters, such as violence committed by militia members, violence committed against police officers, environmental damage, kidnapping, and human trafficking.
9. Confrontations between police and drug dealers in favelas are common in large cities. As a result of these confrontations, uninvolved people are hit by gunfire, often fatally.

10. The names of the public defenders are fictitious to protect their identities. However, I am aware that the family members involved in the cases and other activists may identify them through their statements. Empathy and Honesty were the qualities I observed in them.

Works Cited

Adorno, Sérgio. "Crise no sistema de justiça criminal." *Ciencia e Culture*, vol. 54, no. 1, 2002, pp. 50–51.

Agamben, Giorgio. *Homo Sacer*. Routledge, 2004.

Bell, Derrick. *Silent Covenants: Brown v. Board of Education and the Unfulfilled Hopes for Racial Reform*. Oxford University Press, 2004.

Bonilla-Silva, Eduardo. "Rethinking Racism: Toward a Structural Interpretation." *American Sociological Review*, vol. 62, 1997, pp. 465–80.

Cano, Ignacio. Letalidade da ação policial no Rio de Janeiroo. ISER, 1997.

Carvalho, Deize. *Vencendo as Adversidades: Autobiografia de Deize Carvalho*. Nós por Nós, 2014.

Crenshaw, Kimberlé. "De-marginalizing the Intersection of Race and Sex: A Black Feminist Critique of Anti-discrimination Doctrine, Feminist theory and Anti-racist Policy." *University of Chicago Legal Forum*, 1989, pp. 139–68.

Cunha, Jose Ricardo, editor. *Direitos Humanos e Sistema de Justiça: Uma pesquisa empírica com defensores públicos e promotores de justiça no Rio de Janeiro*. Grandma, 2013.

Delgado Bernal, Dolores. "Critical Race Theory, Latino Critical Theory, and Critical Raced Gendered Epistemologies: Recognizing Students of Color as Holders and Creators of Knowledge." *Qualitative Inquiry*, vol. 8, no. 1, 2002, pp. 105–26.

Delgado, Richard, and Jean Stefancic, editors. *Critical Race Theory: The Cutting Edge*. 2nd ed. Temple University Press, 2000.

Dixson, Adrienne D., and Celia K. Rousseau. *Critical Race Theory in Education: All God's Children Got a Song*. Routledge, 2006.

Farias, Juliana, and Adriana Vianna. "A Guerra das Mães: Dor e Política em Situações de Violência Institucional." *Cadernos Pagu*, vol. 37, 2011, pp. 79–116.

Feagin, Joe. *Systemic Racism: A Theory of Oppression*. Routledge, 2006.

Graham, Barbara Luck. "Toward a Critical Race Theory in Political Science: A New Synthesis for Understanding Race, Law, and Politics." *African American Perspectives on Political Science*. Edited by C.R. Wilbur. Temple University, 2007, pp. 212–31.

Greene, Linda. "Race in the Twenty-First century: Equality through Law?" *Critical Race Theory: The Key Writings that Formed the Movement*. Edited by Kimberlé Crenshaw et al. The New Press, 1995, pp. 292–301.

Harris, Cheryl. "Whiteness as Property." *Critical Race Theory: The Key Writings that Formed the Movement*. Edited by Kimberlé Crenshaw et al. The New Press, 1995, pp. 276–291.

Kant de Lima, Roberto. *Ensaios de antropologia do direito – Acesso à justiça e processos institucionais de administração de conflitos e produção da verdade jurídica em uma perspectiva comparada*. Lumen Juris, 2008.

Lopes Jr., Aury. *Direito Processual Penal e sua conformidade constitucional*. 3rd ed. Lumen Juris, 2010.

McCall, Leslie. "The Complexity of Intersectionality," *Signs*, vol. 30, no. 3, 2005, pp. 1771–1800.

Nascimento, Abdias. *Sitiado Em Lagos: Autodefesa de Um Negro Acossado Pelo Racismo. Rio de Janeiro*. Nova Fronteira, 1981.

Nascimento, Abdias. O Genocídio Do Negro Brasileiro: Processo de Um Racismo Mascarado. Coleção Estudo Brasileiros. Paz e Terra, 1978.

Nash, Jennifer. "Re-thinking Intersectionality." *Feminist Review*, vol. 89, no. 1, 2008, pp. 1–15.

Oliveira, Marcus Vinicius Berno, and Bruno Amaral Machado. "O fluxo do sistema de justiça como técnica de pesquisa no campo da segurança pública." *Rev. Direito Práx*, vol. 9, no. 2, 2018, pp. 781–809.

Pires, Thula Rafaela de Oliveira, and Caroline Lyrio. "Racismo institucional e acesso à justiça: uma análise da atuação do Tribunal de Justiça do Estado do Rio de Janeiro nos anos de 1989-2011." Acesso à justiça I. Edited by M.B. Couto et al. Conpedi, 2014, pp. 1–29.

Rifiotis, Theophilus. "Reflexões críticas sobre a metodologia do estudo do fluxo de justiça criminal em casos de homicídios dolosos." *Revista de Antropologia*, vol. 53, no. 2, 2010, pp. 689–714.

Roberts, Dorothy E. "Punishing Drug Addicts Who Have Babies: Women of Color, Equality, and the Right of Privacy." *Critical Race Theory: The*

Key Writings that Formed the Movement. Edited by Kimberlé Crenshaw et al. The New Press, 1995, pp. 384–425.

Rocha, Luciane O. "Maternidad indignada: Reflexiones sobre el activismo de las madres negras y el uso de las emociones en investigación activista." *Anthropologica*, vol. 36, no. 41, 2018, pp. 35–46.

Sapori, Luis Flávio. "A justiça criminal brasileira como um sistema frouxamente articulado." *Novas direções na governança da justiça e da segurança*. Edited by Catherine Slakmon, et al. Ministério da Justiça, 2006, pp. 763–82.

Silva, Luís Antônio Machado da. "Criminalidade violenta: por uma nova perspectiva de análise." *Revista de Sociologia e Política*, no. 13, 1999, pp. 115–24.

Silva, Klarissa, and Ludmila Ribeiro. Fluxo do Sistema de Justiça Criminal Brazileiro: Um Balanço da Leitura. Cadernos de Segurança Pública. Ano 2. Numero 1. Agosto de 2010.

Solórzano, Daniel. G., and Delores Delgado Bernal. "Examining Transformational Resistance through a Critical Race and LatCrit Theory Framework: Chicana and Chicano Students in an Urban Context." *Urban Education*, vol. 36, no. 3, 2001, pp. 308–42.

Taylor, Edward. "A Primer on Critical Race Theory." *The Journal of Blacks in Higher Education*, no. 19, 1998, pp. 122–24.

VARGAS, João H.C. Julho 2010. "A Diáspora Negra Como Genocídio: Brasil, Estados Unidos ou Uma Geografia Supranacional da Morte e Suas Alternativas". Revista da ABPN. vol. 1, no.2, pp. 31–65.

Vargas, Joana Domingues, and Juliana Neves Rodrigues. "Controle e cerimônia: o inquérito policial em um sistema de justiça criminal frouxamente ajustado." *Soc. State*, vol. 26, no. 1, 2011, pp. 77–96.

Vianna, Adriana. "Etnografando documentos: uma antropóloga em meio a processos judiciais. In: Sergio Ricardo Rodrigues Castilho; Antonio Carlos de Souza Lima; Carla Costa Teixeira." *Antropologia das Práticas de Poder: reflexões etnográficas sobre burocratas, elites e corporações*. Edited by Sergio Ricardo Rodrigues Castilho et al. ContraCapa / LACED, 2014, pp. 43–70.

Zuberi, Tukufu. "Critical Race Theory of Society." *Connecticut Law Review*, vol. 43, 2011, pp. 1573-1591.

24.

The Revolution Will Be Black, Queer, and Mother Led: Reflections on Seven Years of Mothering

Pascale Ife Williams and Johnaé Strong

Foreword

Our journey began many years before our first meeting. We were being shaped as mothers, women, and human beings living in the United States in unique yet similar ways, leading us to the politics that ground our story. Ife existed as a Black mixed-race queer "artivist," sister, space holder, student, and educator born and raised in the Humboldt Park neighbourhood of Chicago. Johnaé existed as a young Black woman, student, youth worker, and artist born in Cleveland and raised in several places throughout the Midwest.

It was evident in our first meeting that Ife loved her city; it was and still is home, something worth fighting for. Johnaé was very much searching for home, love, healing, and something to believe in. She was coming off the heels of physical and emotional displacement as a daughter of parents with substance abuse problems. She had shifted households, states, and school systems and was now a young unwed mother to a Black boy. Our meeting was the bedrock for building a new foundation of a place to call home—a reason to have something worth living for. And there were our babies: two amazingly bright, curious, and deeply emotional Black boys, who were always with their mamas, always in rooms talkin' bout the nature of oppression and the future of Black folks.

The journey of building our sisterhood was strengthened by the will to raise our children as liberated beings while creating a world just enough to accept their freedom. As leaders within the Movement for Black Lives and members of BYP100, we were birthing new versions of ourselves, which sometimes seemed contradictory to the socialized norms of society and the inner systems of our political space. At first, we were the only ones bringing children into the organizing meetings, which lasted hours into the evening. Family and friends would question our decision to be so active and cautioned us against neglecting our children to be "in the movement." We found salvation in our intimate moments processing these charges and venting about the irony of our presence being either a distraction from our mothering or the momentum of the organizing space.

The intimate reflections we offer hold revolutionary mothering—while at times deeply terrifying—as intensely purposeful, daringly tender, and fuelled by expansive imagination. We have come to understand every social unrest, interpersonal, and climate catastrophe as a call to parent in a revolutionary way. While giving guidance is key to parenting, the process of revolutionary mothering is deeply woven in the rhythmic and ritualistic dance of co-learning—from parent to child, child to parent, parent to parent, and child to child. That is learning to be vulnerable and address a question that your child brings to the table sometimes before you believe them or yourself to be ready. That is allowing yourself the full spectrum of error and growth that exists in personhood. That is, falling, falling, and falling but stepping up, hands forward, your village reaching back. Because at the core of every child's gentle, radical, loving, curious, and defiant moments is an adult, or collective of adults, whose sole purpose is to pour knowledge, energy, and life force into that child.

We believe our decision to ground our mothering in the movement was not a surrender of our parenting, nor was bringing our children into those spaces a distraction from our strategic focus. We understood, on an intimate level, that holding life in your arms while strategizing about the futurity of Black life gave even more clarity around our conditions and the stakes of our actions. Raising our children in a space of radical commitment to Black life was affirming our children's worthiness. We knew the creation of a liberated world depended on us being in relationship to the full experience of our lives when anti-Black, patriarchal, racial capitalist, and fascist systems would rather compartmentalize our humanness until each part became smaller and smaller into nonexistence. We resisted these notions and over time expanded these ideas for others because we were not able to disentangle the call to action to love our people from the cries of our babies. Weaving our embodied experience through prose and conversational exchange, we hope this writing offers a unique perspective on the invaluable contribution of Black, queer, and unwed mothers to the cultural shifts in Black liberation work that have finally begun to make visible mothering as central to our movements.

This is a *piece* of our story.

Womb Wisdom: From The Other World to Our Children's Lips[1]

We begin our story by honouring our wombs because it is the site of our first home in this world. Our wombs are our babies' first homes. Our wombs are time travellers, alchemists, and creators of new worlds and possibilities. We also acknowledge that due to the impacts of anti-Black patriarchal oppression, for many Black women, our wombs have become homes to grief, trauma, and lost children. This can be especially true for those outside the privileged aesthetic of motherhood, such as our sisters surviving poverty and our trans sisters born without wombs. For us, our embodiment of revolutionary mothering privileges the intricacies and complexities of Black and queer women-identified mothers and honors the important contribution of othermothering, adoptive mothering, and all other structures of parenting outside white dominant constructs of being and practising.

This acceptance welcomes a profound element of the revolutionary mothering dynamic; community mothering and the gifts awarded to children and mothers with a tribe behind them. Community mothering offers so many opportunities for children to practice through their voice, body, and Divine connections. Like our Elders, our children are closest to the other realm and intuitively tap into spirit in profound ways. It's those moments you swear you just heard your deceased Auntie speak blunt truth through the voice of your five-year-old or the visceral response your infant has to your uncle who carries negative energy. Our traditions remind us that the journey from the Other World, to the womb, and to this world is one that is most tenderly shepherded by Elders. Malidoma Patrice Somé writes:

> Throughout children's life in the village there is a strong message that they belong to a community of people who value them almost beyond anything else. It starts when grandparents participate in the birthing and are the first to hold the newborn. Because the newborn is considered a villager who has just arrived from a long trip that started in the land of the ancestors, the people most recognizable to them are the old ones; grandparents look pretty much like those who were left behind. Another reason for the presence of the elderly is that having just arrived, the newborn shares with the grandparents a close proximity to the Other World. Naturally they bond together. (94)

I, Ife, often sit and meditate in deep gratitude on this passage while reflecting on my own child, Kamari's, beautiful birth story. Kamari was unexpectedly born at home in the bathroom, in October 2011 during a Scorpio new moon on the Westside of Chicago. What is most profound about the birth was that their[2] grandmother, my mama, was the first person to receive and guide him through safe passage into this world. Kamari's grandmother, later affectionately called "BuBu," had no prior experience supporting deliveries (save her own three natural births) yet intuitively tapped into the deeply powerful matrilineage of Elder mothers holding the hands of younger ones. Kamari's and my mama's connection and affinity to each other, owls, the moon, and all things love and play continued to blossom.

When my mama transitioned to the Other World in 2017, ancestor reverence, altar keeping, and other practices celebrating our connections to the Source became even more visceral and attuned. Because of all the oppressive systems and beliefs that have tried (but failed) to rip Black folks of our spirituality, I understand these practices as political—as a right that our ancestors have fought for so that they can be handed down and therefore a duty that we are responsible to pass along. Kamari has begun to hold onto these moments, even attuning me to messages that I would have otherwise likely missed. However, when his grandmother first transitioned, those conversations were not always easy:

Kamari: I don't want to live anymore. It's boring.

Ife: Why is it boring?

Kamari: Cuz I wanna be with BuBu. I wanna die so I can be with BuBu in the sky.

Ife: Well, you know K, it's hard not having BuBu here in body anymore, but she's all around us in spirit all the time. You can always call on her. I don't think it's your time to die yet, but when it is, I'm sure you'll meet her in the sky.

While these conversations around death are difficult, like other topics Black parents must have with their children, they have always brought me so much affirmation and confirmation that our children are tuned in and consciously navigating their worlds: "BuBu visited me last night, as a human. She was laying next to me." Then Kamari told me that tonight she was gonna visit me, but transformed as a pillow... so I need to make sure not to sleep on the pillow by the night stand hahaha."

For us, these reflections embody a praxis of revolutionary mothering because they are deeply intimate and exposed. As Black mothers, constantly navigating life and the fear of death, having these powerful conversations with our children is important. Honouring the child-Elder relationship and connection through our children's birth and life is a true gift. The relationships we build, mature, and maintain through trust, be it with blood or chosen family, are critical to sustaining ourselves and our movements. However, we would not be speaking to the full waves and experience of Black mothering without bringing attention to the moments when we are thrust into practices guided by fear, survival, or fierce protection. Those moments we call guerilla mothering.

Guerilla Mothering

We have carried babies on our hips and protest signs over our shoulders as we marched and tucked sleeping toddlers softly into makeshift resting corners when the strategy meetings went over. We have also left early, not joined the action, or taken extended breaks. Revolutionary mothering looks like everyday acts of care, such as bringing extra snacks because you know your comrade has their nibbling[3] this weekend. It can also look like larger defiant acts like being your comrades "on-call" to pick up the children from school for impromptu overnights when you knew you could very well not return home that night after being arrested.

It feels important to name the tensions we faced as mama organizers and the incessant proclamations to stay committed to "the work." It would be a disservice to omit the tangible work that has sustained us and allowed a path for us to stay committed to ourselves, our children, and our sacred work. The two of us met at a critical moment when being a Black mother to a Black child was a fearful thing. The nation had recently heard the news of the acquittal of George Zimmerman for the murder of Trayvon Martin, which gave birth to the creation of our political home, BYP100. It was in those meeting spaces, talkin' strategy, disruption, and our futures for hours, that our bond and our children's bond formed. Today, our sons call each other "brother" and have a little "sister" in Johnaé's daughter Jari. They share chants and meals, community gatherings and soccer practices, and secrets about their mamas when we're not looking.

When we began co-conspiring together in 2014 as mama-organizers in the early years of BYP100, the focus of our political discourse and debate was how to stop police from killing Black people. Internally, there was a range of political beliefs along the spectrum of police reform to the beginnings of a divest-invest framework. Over the course of the first few years after engaging in direct actions and multi-year campaigns to hold police accountable, it became clear our organization was sharpening a commitment to abolish policing and prisons wholesale. Many of us read and even studied under those holding the work of abolition before us, including Angela Davis, Mariam Kaba, and Beth Ritchie. While we did not create the framework for abolition, we galvanized a broad base of people to a call to engage the politics of abolition and imagine what a world without police could be. Like with anything deeply rooted, the struggle to counter cultural assumptions of policing as a contributor to public safety is hard won. Nonetheless, in the unfiltered murmuring of our children, we have found some pieces of information affirming how differently the future must look to allow our babies to be free. These reflections from me, Johnaé, are telling of how brilliantly insightful children of revolutionary mothering are and how we navigate the lifestyle:

> When Akeim was two years old his teacher taught him about all the "helping professions" and when he saw them, he would eagerly point showin' all his teeth.

After seeing an ambulance: "Emergency help! Mommy they helping somebody!"

After seeing blue police lights: "Mommy! Mommy! Emergency help!"

At this time, I didn't want to teach my son hate or ill will even as I understood the political implications of Black people being criminalized by the state. So in this instance, I simply nodded and kept driving.

Then Cleveland happened. I kept my son with me on the last day of the Movement for Black Lives convening held in 2014 in Cleveland, my hometown. After leaving a session, I got a phone alert that a young boy was being stopped by the transit authority, and folks were going to support. This came the day after I'd been stopped twice by police the night before without just cause. On this day, Akeim and I walked over to what was now a crowd surrounding the young boy and transit authority. It was a two-way street median in between, and Akeim and I were standing on the median. The transit authority seemed so intimidated by the presence of so many Black folks that they hurriedly tried to put the young boy in their car. The community would not allow it, and folks linked up arm in arm to prevent the vehicle from moving with the youth. At this point, my son and I bore witness to abuse when one officer (the highest ranked one there) aimlessly pepper sprayed into the now large circle of Black folks. I stood stunned as those affected cursed and screamed but went back to the line holding arms. It was the last thing I saw as Akeim and I ran to our car to get milk from the closest store we could find. As we ran, all I remember is Akeim saying, "We don't like polices mommy?" It broke my heart to hear my son reach to process what he was seeing juxtaposed to his idea of "emergency help." How would I explain?? In the car on the way to the store, Akeim asked again, "The cops don't like us? Are they after us?" My dear god. I said, "The cops don't like us because we are Black, and they may come after us, but I love you and your blackness. Black is beautiful. You are beautiful. We are going to help our family. We gon be alright." The last words were meant to evoke his sense of joy because Akeim loved and still loves that song.[4] I felt so convicted to hold his young mind and the trauma of seeing what he saw and also give him confidence that there is always help—even if it doesn't come from the police.

Since that experience, I welcomed my second child, Jari Alim, into the world with her father and fellow organizer Malik Alim. Akeim became an older sibling, who loves to teach everything he now knows about the world as an eight-year-old. When they see police lights now, Akeim who has been witness to more intrusive and outright abusive police interactions assures his sister everything is okay because we are together. It is not clear to me if Jari's visceral response to police is from intuition or not being taught that police are "community helpers," but by three years old, on the days following George Floyd's murder, she woke up shaking from a dream that lingered:

Jari: I scared.... I dreamed I need to break the jail, and I couldn't broke it.

Akeim: It's okay ya-ya, mommy and "bro bro" are here.

During the 2020 uprisings, I was intentionally not in the streets; I was home with my children cooking meals, painting, and listening to our favorite artists—Burna Boy, Jay Electronica, Kendrick Lamar, Kota the Friend, and Ego Ella May—and having small meals with loved ones.

We both stayed home. It was a moment where we chose to clothe ourselves and our children with joy and send prayers to our comrades fighting for justice amid global pandemic no less. It wasn't a difficult choice to make because we have grown. The political space we belong to has grown to build more breath for folks to step in and out of direct confrontation with the state to honour our dignity and privilege of having breath and the need to live to fight constant death. This truth has been a real unearthing of what could be in the next phase of our movements.

Making the Road

In addition to the ways we were fed by a high level of community and political sharpening, we had to build deeper layers of support for our emotional and spiritual capacity specific to our experience. Here we offer some of the critical forms of mutual support and the most used makeshift systems that emerged in our seven years and counting of mothering.

Village Support for All of the Movement Babies

The clear and simple way we all care for the movement babies is playing with them when mama has to facilitate a meeting, offering them toys, snacks, and pens out of bags to draw and pass the time. This led our political home to adopt an informal childcare model with commitments to having meals, art supplies, and childcare as a staple at meetings as a result of caretakers consistently bringing more babies, toddlers, youth, and nibblings to the space. What emerged from the acceptance of yielding more new life into a space—often dominated by harsh truths and challenging odds, losses, and trauma—was smiles, laughs, and the spontaneity of littles running through the adults in an imaginary game of play. Essentially, the invitation of new life grounds us in hope and possibility—a foundation for the radical imagination.

Mutual Care: The Radical, Black, Queer, Mama Co-op

Our intentional SiStar circles, which include mothering and nonmothering individuals, have allowed us to build the trust to show up for one another in tangible ways. On numerous occasions, we have shared rides, arranged pick up and drop-offs (shout out to Ife's fifteen-year-old hand-me-down car PRINCE), and held space for extended sleepovers when either of us had to work out of town or needed a night off. We've also shared resources, hosted space for each other's celebration of life, showed up to honour the transition of family, and held countless FaceTimes to process everyday living, grieve, share jokes and have twerk circles.

Following the Child

To raise liberated Black children and unlock their potential to imagine for themselves more than what they have been socialized to, we as revolutionary mamas are learning to trust our children. Moving away from the dominant parenting experience many of us had as littles, we have supported one another in easing into more play, more surrender, and more mess (e.g., painting with our babies, blowing bubbles, making big splashes, and trying experimental cooking). Through this effort, we embody a form of creative parenting in which our filters as adults can be disrupted, and we allow ourselves, when appropriate and safe, to be led by the child. This also includes investing in activities and educational spaces to support our children's genius (and co investing as family members to support one another financially by extending financial aid).

In following the child, we are also committing to celebrating them when they are courageous and to celebrating their uniqueness and their power—building our connections together.

Leaning into the Deep

The result of liberatory parenting is liberated children who often challenge all sorts of power dynamics, supported by our commitment to noncorporal and nonpunitive interactions we face at the expense of true expression as littles. This commitment, while challenging to our mental conditioning, is nourishing to our children as well as healing for our inner child. It has stretched our capacity to respond differently, including the following: pausing to breathe before responding to questions; asking questions versus reacting to children's emotions; making compassionate eye contact when they are speaking to really see the heart of them as they practise vulnerability; apologizing when we fall back into yelling or being emotionally reactive, honouring their invitation to stop working and watch a movie or go outside when that deadline feels most important; and breaking open a book and spending quality time when screen time promises mama some quiet time to think. This commitment also creates a real pathway for our children's transformation. As they are presented with predetermined ways of being, such as naming the presence of toxic masculinity with our boys and inviting them to explore if what they said is how they truly feel or when they're fitting into a norm. For example, when Akeim brought home some homophobic language and binary ideas or was embarrassed to admit he wanted to paint his nails. These conversations often have us facing ingrained ideas in our blood families to appeal for solidarity around being inclusive and loving to all the ways our Blackness exists. What we've found is that those talks have strengthened our relationships even when we disagree and helped us as adults to model mutual understanding focused on what makes our children happy as opposed to who is right or wrong on the specific subject. It has given us hope that when adults, movement folks or not, focus on the promise new life brings through children, we can heal past generational traumas and honour our own repressed versions of who we once were and what we believed was possible in our innocence as children.

Returning Home

We hope we have illuminated how the praxis we embody in our everyday lives are drenched in care—from honouring our womb wisdom, our birthing stories and teaching our children practices of ancestral reverence to the heart wrenching conversations we must have with our children about the state of the world. These praxis are core elements to the fight for Black liberation; if we cannot imagine a world where we are able to rest and replenish we are replicating the conditions for further deterioration of the very human element of connection with the self, the universe, and each other.

As young Black and queer unwed mothers, we must commit to constantly coming home to ourselves, to our wombs, to our inner love. We do this to tap into the wisdom we carry through our blood memory to sustain the work it takes to raise tender-hearted, perfectly (imperfect) unabashedly resistant (yet respectful) liberated children. In this, we understand that we must embody for ourselves the practice of care as one of the only ways we can truly practice care for others. This work takes breaking down, falling apart, and coming face-to-face with our shadows in love. It requires that we disrupt any shame we've built up about the precariousness of Black motherhood and any guilt we've embedded in our minds about hauling our children along with us for the fight.

Admittedly, our mothering journey has included multiple moments of breakdown and burnout even amid having a beloved community of care. Alongside care, we sometimes still battle the ways society force-feeds Black, queer, unwed mothers narratives of shame and guilt around pausing. Until, finally, the body, spirit, and emotional senses refuse to move any further no matter the responsibilities that lie in the wake. In those moments, it becomes clear just how urgent a praxis of care is. Our children are so unapologetic about what they need that they call us back into the deeply political necessity of intentional focus to stand in our dignity and in right relationship with ourselves, our earth, and each other.

Endnotes

1. This subtitle is inspired by Malidoma Patrice Somé's *The Healing Wisdom of Africa: Finding Life Purpose Through Nature, Ritual, and Community.*

2. Kamari has been exploring gender fluidity and has asked to use all pronouns. In this chapter, we use he/his and they/their interchangeably.
3. "Nibbling" is a gender-neutral term referring to the children of your siblings/comrades, made popular by adrienne maree brown.
4. "I Love Being Black" was written by our sister-friend and comrade JeNae Taylor and composed by Jonathan Lykes.

Works Cited

Somé, Malidoma Patrice. *The Healing Wisdom of Africa: Finding Life Purpose through Nature, Ritual, and Community.* TarcherPerigee, 1999.

waheed, nayyirah. "A Mother's Love." *Vibe Magazine*, 8 May 2016, https://www.vibe.com/features/digital-covers/afeni-shakur-mothers-day-poem-420884/. Accessed 29 Dec. 2024.

25.

Motherhood in the Land of Hope

Jameka Hartley

"Mommy, I want to see a police car," my four-year-old daughter chirped happily from her car seat.

"A police car?" I responded quizzically.

She nodded her head in affirmation.

I don't remember the response I gave her in an effort to redirect her request. What I remember is the pit in my stomach from her asking.

I suspect that other Black mothers have experienced this same sinking feeling in their gut. Navigating questions like the one above come as part of the "mothering while Black" starter pack, which includes discussing race at an early age, the talk of how to act if a cop pulls you over, and how to deflect from someone touching your hair.

There are distinct aspects of mothering while Black, and one key Black mother and writer Toni Morrison, captured it well during her lifetime. Andrea O'Reilly articulates that Morrison puts forth a "fully developed theory of African American mothering" (1) through both her fiction and her aural and oral reflections on motherhood in interviews. O'Reilly describes Morrison's theory as a "politics of the heart" (1) and further articulates it as a theory of maternal practice, namely motherwork, concerned with the empowerment of children (26). Patricia Hill Collins defines motherwork as follows:

[Motherwork] soften[s] the dichotomies in feminist theorizing about motherhood that posit rigid distinctions between private and public, family and work, the individual and the collective, identity as individual autonomy and identity growing from the collective self-determination of one's group. Racial ethnic women's mothering and work experiences occur at the boundaries demarking these dualities. (373)

O'Reilly defines the scope of Morrison's motherwork theory to be "four distinct yet interrelated tasks: 1) preservation, 2) nurturance, 3) cultural bearing and 4) healing" (26). I believe there is a fifth overarching task: hope. To be a Black mother is to foster a state of hopefulness.

In this autoethnographic chapter, I offer a Black feminist theorization of motherwork. I offer personal stories and imaginings to make sense of the additional labour of mothering while Black using Morrison's motherwork as my theoretical frame. Activist, writer, and educator Mariame Kaba speaks of hope as a discipline. It is with hope in mind and heart that I approach this (mother)work.

Preservation

When I initially started thinking of mothering and motherwork in the time of Black Lives Matter, I immediately thought of encounters with the police state, and statistics such as these are why. According to data shared by the African American Policy Forum via Twitter:

- Nearly 60 per cent of Black women killed by police were unarmed at the time of their death, the most of any raced gender group.
- Black women are at the highest risk of any group to experience sexual violence perpetrated by police officers.
- Black women are 17 per cent more likely to be in a police-initiated traffic stop than white women.
- Black women's imprisonment rate is twice that of white women.
- Black girls are more than three times as likely to be incarcerated than their white peers.

If preservation is about protecting the lives of Black children, I think often of can we truly do that in a police state. The answer I come to is we cannot. Police are venerated within the child media landscape. From *Paw Patrol* to *Sesame Street*, children are taught that police are good and are for them. My oldest daughter still believes the copaganda. Meanwhile, every time we leave our house, I am keenly aware how Black Americans are seen through the eyes of the state. Unteaching the lessons I did not teach is part of the motherwork of preservation.

Nurturance

According to O'Reilly, "The aim of black mothering, once preservation has been ensured, is to nurture children so that they may survive and resist the maiming of racism and, for daughters, sexism and grow into adulthood whole and complete" (32–33). One of the earliest places of potential harm for Black children is at school. Black mothers are aware of the hazards inherent in white patriarchal spaces that often systematically diminish the humanity of Black kids. As a Black mother, education does not begin and end at the school but extends into the home. Nurturance includes being and fostering a homeplace for their children. Homeplace, as defined by bell hooks, refers "to a haven or refuge, where black people could affirm one another and by so doing, heal many of the wounds inflicted by racist domination" (42). At times that homeplace looks like advocacy. That was one of the ways my mother was a homeplace for me as child.

The first time it happened I didn't think it was a big deal. I corrected my teacher and moved on. "I'm Jameka. Not Porsche."

Then it kept happening.

Every day, I'd have to remind my teacher of my name.

That's when I started to feel sad.

Sad that my teacher didn't know my name.

It was evident to me that she only ever mixed my name up with Porsche's, the only other Black girl in class, and no one else's.

When my mom asked me about school one evening, I shared how sad I felt that my teacher kept calling me by the wrong name.

My mom, although visibly bothered, calmly asked me to explain what was happening at school and how long had the teacher been calling me Porsche and not Jameka.

I answered her, and she expressed to me that she'd speak to the teacher and that it would be handled.

My mom did talk to my teacher and the principal of the school. I'm not sure what she said, but I do know that my teacher learned to call me by my name.

Culture Bearing

O'Reilly expands upon Morrison's motherwork theory by explaining that Black "women are the keepers of the tradition ... the culture bearers who mentor and model the values essential to the empowerment of black children and culture" (11). Culture includes ancestral memory, since if Black children "are going to survive they must know the stories, legends, and myths of their ancestors" (12). Black mothers must be intentional in their mothering practices to ensure this passing down of memory and instill a pride and love for their Blackness and Black people. Some of the ways these intentions can be seen are in the media that is consumed, the art in the home, and the family stories shared.

Healing

In her description of healing as motherwork, O'Reilly describes the preservation, nurturance, and culture-bearing functions of motherwork as preventive or proactive acts that empower children to survive and resist (38). She deems Morrison's healing "as a re-active or restorative practice insofar as it seeks to repair selfhood that has been displaced or damaged by the hurts of a racist and a patriarchal culture" (38). As a white mother, O'Reilly formulates this healing as reactive or restorative; as a Black mother, I see it as proactive and preventative and necessary. To see Black maternal healing as reactive centres whiteness, trauma, and pain inflicted by racism, sexism, patriarchy, etc. To see Black maternal healing as proactive centres Blackness, love, and the sanctity of life. O'Reilly also posits that the first three themes are proactive because they empower children to survive and resist. Yet surviving and resisting are not the dream Black mothers have for their children. We want our children to move beyond mere survival to thriving.

Preservation is reactionary to white supremacist capitalist patriarchy. When you have to literally declare that your life and the lives of your children and community matter, that is not restorative, especially in the face of ongoing Black death and trauma. Alicia Garza, Patrisse Cullors, and Opal Tometi cofounded Black Lives Matter as a new, fresh path towards Black liberation—one that did not diminish preexisting institutions, such as the NAACP or Urban League, but one that opened emergent possibilities of abolition and care.

While the police state and Black Lives Matter are intertwined in many ways. Morrison's transformative motherwork creates nonlinear ways of thinking about how to curate livable lives for our children by abiding in a productive liminal space of the past and future simultaneously. Transformative justice is about the materiality of Black Life. Black Breathe. Black people in wholeness. Patrisse Cullors explains in a 2020 interview that as a society we have "prioritized punishment, humiliation, public shaming and the tortured killing of Black people through the police state" and that through the portal of abolition we can "invest in Black life." Abolition does not end at the dismantling of the police state, but it does offer us a beginning. When I dream of what a possible beginning could look like I see systemic communal care.

Vision

"Hey, is everything okay? Do you need me to call the police?" an older woman asked. A teenage girl was doubled over.

The young girl's knees were tucked under her chin.

"The police?" she lifted her head, confused. "Uhh, do you mean the community carer?"

"Oh, yes, the community carer. I'm sorry. I was thinking of the before times," she said, as she scratched her head seemingly lost in thought.

"Um, ma'am, are you okay?" the young girl inquired.

"Goodness, I stopped to check on you, and here you are tending to me! My apologies! I'm fine, just lost in memories is all. It happens as you age." She smiled.

Youthful eyes smiled in return.

"I've gotten lost in my thoughts. Do you need me to make the call?" the older woman asked again.

"Yes, please. That would be helpful. I also need to call my mom. She's probably worried that I haven't checked in."

"Yes of course. Let's call her first then," the woman offered.

"Ok. Thank you." The girl exhaled a relieving breath and unfurled her legs.

Hope

Mothering in the times of Black Lives Matter is both historical and ancestral. Black mothers have always been calling attention to the lives of themselves and their children from the times of chattel slavery to the Civil Rights Movement to present day. Black mothers have been wrestling with and creating pathways forged in hope to more liberated living for centuries.

Mariame Kaba explained in a 2018 interview that hope is not an emotion or optimism but is something that we must practice daily. She clarifies that hope does not "preclude feeling sadness or frustration or anger or any other emotion"; instead, it is a discipline to look at the world with hopeful eyes and "choose to think a different way." When hope is a discipline, one can "believe there are more people who want justice ... than there are those who are working against [it]" (qtd. in Sonenstein and Wilson). Black mothers know full well the odds facing their children but to believe anything less than change is possible would be sentencing their children to toil and death. It is in the daily enactment of liberatory hope that Black mothers can work towards and for preservation, nurturance, culture bearing, and healing. And do it all in love.

Works Cited

@AAPolicyForum. "We must #SayHerName to End State Violence against Black women. Here Are 5 Things to Know about the Impact of State Violence on Black women in the US Today." X, 24 Mar. 2021, 12:39 p.m., https://x.com/aapolicyforum/status/1374777861496799234?lang=ar&mx=2. Accessed 30 Dec. 2024.

Collins, Patricia Hill. "Shifting the Center: Race, Class and Feminist Theorizing about Motherhood." *Representations of Motherhood*. Edited by Donna Bassin. Yale University Press, 1994, pp. 371–89.

"Creativity and Leadership with Patrisse Cullors." *Finding Our Way* from Prentiss Hemphill, 7 September 2020, https://www.findingourway-podcast.com/individual-episodes/sle4

hooks, bell. *Yearning: Race, Gender, and Cultural Politics*. Routledge. 2015.

Sonenstein, Brian, and Kim Wilson. "Hope Is a Discipline feat. Mariame Kaba." *Beyond Prisons*, 5 Jan. 2018, https://www.beyond-prisons.com/home/hope-is-a-discipline-feat-mariame-kaba. Accessed 30 Dec. 2024.

O'Reilly, Andrea. *Toni Morrison and Motherhood: A Politics of the Heart*. State University of New York Press, 2004.

26.

My Afro-Cultural Renaissance

Azenia Whitaker

I learned a lot about Blackness
this year.
I learned a lot about hope

And empathy.

I learned a lot about fear.

I reacquainted myself with my past.
Almost joyfully,
as tragic as it was.

(Not just for me
but for everyone who looked like me.)

How could I not know
The things I didn't know
About Black people?
How they lived.
How they died.
Who they were.
And what they left us.

AZENIA WHITAKER

How could I not know?

I do know I'm not the only one
Who got felt up by my mother's white landlord
In the hallway of my house
On rent day.
I was eleven years old.

I know I'm not the only one
Who was a product of segregation
In a 1970s small Texas town
Who sat in a classroom
With my head down.
Not afraid
Just unaware of my potential.

I know I'm not the only one
Who walked away with a degree
In triviality
But failed to see
And declined to take advantage
Of the benefits
Of an education that was free
At the time.

I know I'm not the only Black mother
Who rescued her children
Time and again from injustice
Without realizing the why of it all
Who let the opportunity
To teach what I did know
Slip into the creek.

How could I not know?

I realized

that I wasn't Black
Back then.
There was no ownership
Of my Black experience.
No acceptance of the rich heritage
That was duly mine by birth.
A product of the masses
Without definition.

Today, I am a Queen.

I am still studying
BLACK LIVES MATTER

Not its historical significance.
But its relevance.
Its power as a statement.
Its simplicity.
Its movement.

Knowing this history
Is like a breath
of soul
Returning to my body.

An elixir daily
That fortifies me like Geritol.
I can breathe deeply
With my chest stuck out with pride,
As I tell my offspring

What I know now.

27.

Soiled Bandanas

Toya Leigh Groves

soiled bandanas
breath back debris
war particulate in matters
coloured by death did he really
hold a knife and threaten the
breath? of fruited wombs
of daughters and mothers outta line
and out on the line scream *I would
take a bullet for mine!*
but was he yours?
or did he cast himself astray
whitened by prey
life kneed upon
calling now for Mama
daughters hold the picture in minds
the whole wide world watching
stopping
breath
Karma called upon
death

28.

at the march for George Floyd

Toya Leigh Groves

masks and marches crowded faiths bumping. hips on a burning building. chanting lips through rage chapped feelin'. hollerin. names disgraced by pigs. boots tied up with lynch rope laces. marching over redneck faces. wrinkled sunlight. youth left traces. smeared sea me eye and eye to I. blooding the sky. greeting night with black smoked high. left and looted through. broken
    boxes emptied a stolen shoe. scattered and tore across the floor. soldiers roar. the day marching boots and running shoes. rallied on and through … to save the world … we gave it back to you.

spread legs opened wide. stretched and pulled from inside. birthed riots. lipped guns. cocked and clipped. GTA from Klan land corners. walls pulled down and under borders. bottles turned and cocktail fire squads. and blackened soul prints on paper. ink and paint. immunized by vaper. tears peppered over cheek and bone. murders hanging on to phone calls. the rushing dead marching on and through.

forced fed we gave it back to you.

punched and jabbed and blackened I. bruises welts. a firefly. a lightning string severed the bound. ungagged the call. prayers and rage bang on concrete walls. the day the world saw it all. caught in shaking hands. reflections memoried in tears. running down and out. youngster gazed brown-pooled eyes. white sockets breathing in. caught the devil kneed in sin. red-handed caught in molted mud. and gave it back written in blood. crossing fifty states resurrected. burnt and blazed by mamas' gun.

29.

The Dead Have a Voice

Luciane Rocha

The image shows Ana Lucia de Oliveira and Dalva da Silva, two mothers of victims of violence in Rio de Janeiro, Brazil. They are preparing mannequins to be dressed and covered in red paint to represent the killing of young Black men. Their motherhood does not end when their children are killed. They continue to take care of them by protesting to denounce police brutality.

30.

Investigate!

Luciane Rocha

The picture shows family members who lost loved ones to police brutality from different favelas in Rio de Janeiro, Brazil. They protest against the slowness of the civil police, who are responsible for investigating the cases. Many cases extend for decades without resolution. This situation results in mental and physical illness for family members, especially mothers. Janaina Andrade (the fourth woman from right to left)—and the mother of Cristian de Andrade, who was killed by the police at thirteen—died days after this protest due to the pain of having her child killed by the militarized forces of the Brazilian state. Cristian was playing soccer in Manguinhos favela when police officers arrived and started shooting.

Notes on Contributors

Adriel Michelle Barnett (b. Brooklyn, NY) is a Jamaican American photo-based artist whose work explores identity, heritage, mythology, and belonging within the Afro-Caribbean diaspora. In 2024, she completed the one-year certificate program in creative practice at the International Center of Photography to focus on impactful photographic storytelling. That same year, she was a finalist in the Lucie Foundation's Heritage Awards (black-and-white category). Her recent work on family has been included in group exhibitions and featured in The Guardian. Her book, Her Odyssey of Light, was recently published by Snap Collective.

Shana Calixte-Pitawanakwat lives on the unceded territory of the Anishinaabe peoples in Northern Ontario, Canada. She is the director of health equity at Ontario Health North Regions and has experience in the public health and mental health sectors. A former sessional lecturer at Thorneloe University, she focussed on gender studies, embodied research, and mothering pedagogies. Following the university's closure in 2021, she became an honorary fellow. With over twenty-five years of community leadership, Shana uses her lived experience to drive her work and has been recognized as one of Canadian Living Magazine's forty women change makers.

Haile Eshe Cole has a BA in sociology and African American studies and an MA and a PhD in cultural anthropology from the University of Texas at Austin. Over the years, Haile has conducted research on alternatives to incarceration for mothers and their children in both Texas and New York, as well as maternal and infant mortality for Black women.

She has served on the faculty at a number of academic institutions teaching courses on reproductive health, film/media, and other social justice topics. Currently, she is an assistant professor at Central Connecticut State University.

Dawn Demps is an assistant professor at Arizona State University in educational policy and evaluation. Her scholarship focusses on anti-Blackness, school-community relationships, and educational grassroots organizing. She is a Black mother-bridge-interrupter-scholar who has been involved with community advocacy and organizing since she was twelve years old.

Devynity is a visual artist and writer from Queens, NY, whose work makes the trajectory of the African diasporic heritage, experience, and legacy prominent. Wray was a Nuyorican Poet's Café Grand Slam finalist and team member in 2002. Her poem "Black Girl Manifesto" was published in Hill Harper's *Letters to a Young Sister*. Wray's artwork has been exhibited in group shows in New York and New Jersey. She is currently in pursuit of an MFA in visual art at Lesley University.

Cynthia Rachel Esperança, also known as Cynthia Rachel Pereira Lima, has a degree in performing arts and is a playwright. She has a Master's degree from the Postgraduate Program in Culture and Territorialities (PPCULT) at the Universidade Federal Fluminense (UFF). She has an undergraduate degree in Portuguese letters and literature from Universidade Castelo Branco. She created the Encruzilhada Feminina de Arte Negra Collective, for which she writes, directs and produces theatre shows. She works in literature, theatre, cinema, storytelling, curating, and art workshops for children. Since 2018, she has been writing for the Preto no Palco project, created by photographer Valmyr Ferreira. She has contributed to literary anthologies and written *Mulheres Memórias e Afins-Até o fim* and the children's book *O Menino Omolu*.

Erica Ewa-Elechi's struggle for Black liberation stems from her lived experiences as a Black woman growing up in Ottawa, Canada. She aims to speak up for Black life through avenues of research, education and community capacity building. As a MSW graduate, Erica's research, titled *Reproduction of Anti-Black Racism within Child Welfare*, focussed on how anti-Black racism manifests itself within this system of power by centring the experiences of a Black child welfare survivor.

NOTES ON CONTRIBUTORS

Stephanie Fearon is an arts-informed narrative researcher. Her research focuses on Black motherhood as well as educational leadership and policy. Dr. Fearon's work uses literary and visual arts to communicate, in a structured, creative, and accessible form, insights gleaned from stories shared by Black Canadian mothers.

Toya Leigh Groves is a teacher and writer who currently works with formerly incarcerated students at Laney College in Oakland, California. She holds a BA in African American studies from UC Berkeley, an MA in women's spirituality from Sofia University, and an MFA in creative writing from Mills College. Her role as a single mother of two daughters and one son is an honour that she beholds as her highest. Her writing includes attributes revealing the challenges and rewards of her journey that include surviving domestic violence, rape, abandonment, homelessness, and disability while also highlighting the victory of forgiving herself and those who once trespassed against her. After losing the use of her right dominant hand in a car accident, she relearned to write and navigate the world as a Black person and woman literally single handedly. It is her life's work to illuminate the dark by telling the story of Black motherhood as she sees and experiences it. She hopes to inspire other mothers to raise their voices in chants for healing, love, and freedom.

Johari Harris is a research assistant professor at the University of Virginia who examines how social identities, specifically race and gender, along with cultural values systems, like Afro-centric values, influence African American adolescents' social-emotional competencies. Her research is grounded in intersectionality, developmental psychology, and social psychology theories.

Joshua Harris is a Black queer organizer, activist, and child welfare survivor/abolitionist. Josh's work centres on the intersections of Blackness, disability and madness, child welfare survivorship, queerness, and transness. Josh's research titled *From Topic and Evidence to Architect: The Development of Black Diasporic Interpretive Phenomenology and the Resistive Strategies of Black Child Welfare Survivors*, received Toronto Metropolitan University's Graduate Writers Award in 2019. Joshua's doctoral research addresses the question of whether the experiences and outcomes of Black children into white households for legal adoption reflect Black children's best interests, protection, and wellbeing.

Jameka Hartley, PhD, is an interdisciplinary Black feminist scholar and poet. Her work centres on issues of Black motherhood, popular cultural representations of Black women, child-to-adult outcomes, and stigma. Her simultaneous identities of being a daughter and a mother shape her life and her scholarship.

Alexis Henderson identifies as a single Black mother. She states the following about herself: "I've learned to be resilient. I've learned to lean and depend on the almighty to bring me through any situation. I was blessed with writing, and my dreams are to make a difference. I want to touch as many souls as I can. I want to teach my children to make a change and lead with love. I want to be the change I want to see in the world."

Seanna Leath is an assistant professor at the University of Virginia whose scholarship focusses on the holistic development and cultural resilience of Black girls and women in the context of families, schools, and communities. A number of her current projects focus on Black family processes—and more specifically—how Black mothers try to prepare and protect their children from racialized and gendered bias.

Alana Lim obtained her BS in microbiology from the University of Washington, Seattle. She is currently an associate scientist at Just-Evotec Biologics in Seattle, WA.

Heather Lynch is a photographer and filmmaker born and raised in New York City. She has always been passionate about using her camera to empower those around her and deeply understands the complexities of beauty and representation. As a first-generation Trinidadian American living in Bed-Stuy, Brooklyn, Heather draws from her own experiences to honour her subjects using her sacred lens to create a space where they are free of stereotypes and can create their own identities. She is committed to shifting the misrepresentation of marginalized communities, starting with those in her community. Her work is characterized by a deep empathy for her subjects and a commitment to representing them in a way that is authentic and empowering.

Ayan Mohamed obtained her BA in public health and her Master's in public health from the University of Washington, Seattle. She is a former community health fellow with the American Public Health Association and Kaiser Permanente (Grady Health System in Atlanta, Georgia, 2023-2024). Ayan is dedicated to drawing upon lived experiences, research, and practice to create community-based approaches to dismantle barriers to healthcare access.

Chelsi West Ohueri is a sociocultural anthropologist and assistant professor of Slavic and Eurasian studies at the University of Texas at Austin. Her research examines race, racialization, and marginalization in the Balkans. She additionally conducts research on structural inequality and health. Her current book project explores racialization and racial belonging in Albania.

LaShawnDa Pittman is an associate professor in the Department of American Ethnic Studies at the University of Washington. She is the Joff Hanauer Honors Professor in Western Civilization and has an appointment in the Department of Sociology. She is the author of *Grandmothering While Black: A Twenty-First Century Story of Love, Coercion and Survival* and the founder and director of the Black digital humanities projects—The Black Grandmother Archive and The Black Grandmother Worldmaking Library.

Luciane Rocha has a BA in social sciences from the Federal University of Rio de Janeiro, Brazil, and an MA and a PhD in anthropology from the University of Texas at Austin. She specializes in African and African diaspora studies and gender and women's studies. Her PhD dissertation, *Outraged Mothering: Black Women, Racial Violence and the Power of Emotions in Rio de Janeiro's African Diaspora*, examines the activism of mothers whose lives have been affected by violence in Brazil. Currently, she is an assistant professor and program coordinator for the Black studies program at Kennesaw State University.

Christina Santi is a multimedia journalist whose work centers on advocating for the equality and equity of Black people—particularly Black women, and the complex waters of navigating the intersectionality of race and gender. Her work has appeared in BNC and EBONY magazine, where she was nominated for a GLAAD Award for coverage of the LGBTQ community. A Bronx native, Christina can be found at home with her young son, listening to Frank Ocean and dissecting James Baldwin's work.

Mia Schuman obtained her BA in gender, women, and sexuality studies from the University of Washington, Seattle. She works at the University of California San Francisco Medical Center in obstetrics and gynecology helping pregnant patients and their families coordinate a prenatal care program. In 2025, she will attend the University of Michigan to obtain her Master's in social work and explore her interests of reproductive health, pediatric mental health, and adverse childhood experiences.

Johnaé Strong is a writer, healer, and creative based in Chicago, Illinois. She has a background in education and international studies and has spent the past ten years in social movement organizing. Her work integrates political education, healing, and organizing with a focus on Black girls. Her greatest work is her children: Akeim and Jari. Johnaé is on all social media @strong_visions

Rachel Vulk obtained her BS in environmental science and resource management from the University of Washington, Seattle. She works as a water quality specialist at the Texas Commission on Environmental Quality in Austin, Texas. Rachel is committed to working at the intersection of social and environmental justice, research, writing, and creativity.

Azenia Whitaker was born and raised in central Texas. She now resides in New England near her two daughters and grandchildren. She received her Bachelor's in radio, television, and film from the University of Texas in Austin and has a Master's degree in education. Creatively, she has a passion for writing and theatre and has received honours for her poetry and theatre performances. Professionally, she has devoted her life to educating young people and is a retired schoolteacher of over twenty years.

Pascale Ife Williams is a Black mixed-race queer cultural educator, healer justice practitioner, disruptor and space creator. She is a Chicago native with over 15 years in community practice, which explores and complicates racial, gender, and wellness equity. Her tribe is most precious, especially her child Kamari—a constant source of humility, inspiration, and laughter. Williams currently works as a visiting faculty in arts administration and policy at the School of the Art Institute of Chicago.

Traci-Ann Wint is an assistant professor of Africana studies at Smith College. She holds a PhD in AADS and an MA in anthropology both from UT Austin. Her research explores the ways a neocolonial tourism industry extends the raced and gendered hierarchies of the plantation in the modern anglophone Caribbean.

Rina Yan earned her BA in public health from the University of Washington, Seattle. She is currently a medical student at the Washington State University Elson S. Floyd College of Medicine, with a strong commitment to advancing healthcare equity and addressing health disparities.

Deepest appreciation to
Demeter's monthly Donors

Daughters
Heather Olson Beal
Carole Trainor
Khin May Kyawt
Tatjana Takseva
Debbie Byrd
Tanya Cassidy
Myrel Chernick
Marcella Gemelli
Donna Lee, In Memory of Dee Stark, RN, LNHA,
Trailblazer for Women, Women's Rights Advocate
Catherine Cheleen-Mosqueda

Sisters
Fiona Green
Paul Chu
Amber Kinser
Nicole Willey

Mother
Mildred Bennett Walker (Trainor)

Grandmother
Tina Powell